Cover artwork by
Mike Ray

Created and Designed by
David Salariya

Editor
Jamie Pitman

Published in Great Britain MMXIII by
Book House, an imprint of
The Salariya Book Company Ltd
25 Marlborough Place, Brighton, BNI IUB
www.salariya.com
www.book-house.co.uk

1 3 5 7 9 8 6 4 2
ISBN 978-1-908973-40-5
A CIP catalogue record for this book is available
from the British Library.

Printed and bound in India.
Printed on paper from sustainable sources.

Visit
www.salariya.com
for our online catalogue and
free interactive web books.

HEROES, GODS AND MONSTERS OF

ANCIENT GREEK MYTHOLOGY

BY MICHAEL FORD

ILLUSTRATED BY EOIN COVENEY

HEROES, GODS AND MONSTERS OF ANCIENT GREEK MYTHOLOGY

MICHAEL FORD

EOIN COVENEY

BOOK HOUSE

BRIGHTON
MMXIII

INTRODUCTION: 11
A Short History of
Ancient Greece

CHAPTER I: 25
The War of the Titans

CHAPTER II: 31
Jason and the Argonauts

CHAPTER III: 61
Theseus and the Minotaur

CHAPTER IV: 77
The Twelve Labours of
Heracles

CHAPTER V: 93
The Curse of Thebes

CHAPTER VI: 103
Perseus and Medusa

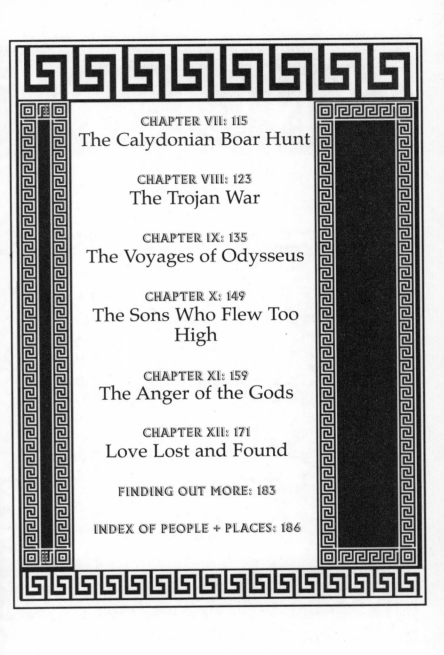

CHAPTER VII: 115
The Calydonian Boar Hunt

CHAPTER VIII: 123
The Trojan War

CHAPTER IX: 135
The Voyages of Odysseus

CHAPTER X: 149
The Sons Who Flew Too
High

CHAPTER XI: 159
The Anger of the Gods

CHAPTER XII: 171
Love Lost and Found

FINDING OUT MORE: 183

INDEX OF PEOPLE + PLACES: 186

ANCIENT

MACEDONIA

EPIRUS

Mt OLYMPUS

THESSALY

Corcyra

Leuca
Ithaca

EUBOEA

ACHAIA

PELOPONNESUS

o Sparta

Cythara

GREECE

THRACE

Byzantium

Thasos

PHRYGIA

MYSIA

Lesbos

LYDIA

Chios

Samos

CARIA

Miletus

Naxos

RHODES

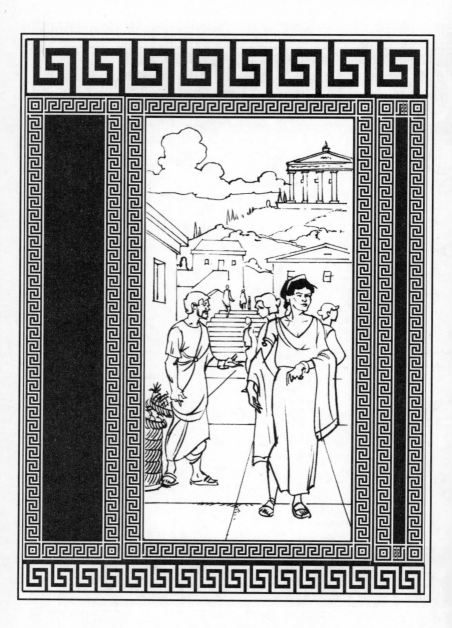

INTRODUCTION

A SHORT HISTORY OF ANCIENT GREECE

People have lived in Greece for thousands of years, but we know little about them before 1100 BC, as almost all of their buildings, writings and artworks have been lost to us. From archaeological digs, we know that a race called the Minoans lived on the island of Crete before 1000 BC, and that they were probably the most powerful race in the Mediterranean at that time.

It is likely that invasions from a race called the Dorians, and possibly a catastrophic natural disaster, cast the Greek world into turmoil around 1100 BC. The next three hundred years have come to be known as the Greek Dark Ages, because we do not know very much about them. The art of writing[1] came to an end, so we have no written records telling us about daily life or historical events. Certainly, there is evidence that the once-proud Minoan civilisation was all but wiped out at around this time.

It is only after about 800 BC that we really come to recognise Ancient Greece as an historic civilisation in its own right. The period from 800 BC to 500 BC is known as the 'Archaic Period'. At this time, the different populations living on the mainland and the surrounding islands began to form into what we call 'city-states'. These communities governed themselves, traded with one another, and were ruled by lords or kings. Importantly, though, most shared

---

1. At this time, the ancient Greeks used a script
   known to archaeologists as 'Linear B'.

certain things in common: they spoke the same language and worshipped the same family (or Pantheon) of Gods.

In this period, we see the flourishing of literature, architecture and other art forms in the Greek city-states. The most powerful of these centres of culture were the city-states of Sparta and Athens. For hundreds of years, these two were on-and-off enemies, forming alliances with other city-states in their quest for dominance. In the 5th century BC they joined forces to fight off a huge invasion from the mighty kingdom of Persia. But this conflict was the beginning of the end for the Greeks. Over the next one hundred and fifty years, although the arts still flourished, Athens and Sparta became less powerful.

In the 4th century BC a visionary commander called Philip of Macedonia,[1] brought the Greek city-states together under his control. His son, Alexander the Great, continued the conquest east into Persia and

1. *A region north of modern Greece.*

beyond to the land we now call India. But after his death, the empire was too large for one ruler to control. It gradually fell to pieces as other cultures, such as the mighty Roman Republic,[1] took control of Greek lands. The country still had its own language and identity, but as a powerful nation, it was to be no more.

1. *A place not ruled by a king, but by a group of elected officials.*

Everyday life in Ancient Greece

The geography of Greece is varied, with many islands, mountains and remote natural harbours. The difficulties of travel in ancient times meant that the Greek world was divided into city-states. Most people would have been farmers, rearing crops and animals in order to feed their families. Anything left over could be swapped or sold.

That isn't to say that there weren't other professions: craftsmen would make ceramics, tradesmen would import goods and sell them at market, wine growers would tend their vineyards and actors would perform in the theatre. Carpenters would make furniture, teachers would instruct the young, there were physicians to heal, and priests would look after the many ornate temples to the Greek Gods. Most of the information we have is about the powerful city-state of Athens, where there was a thriving culture of arts, politics, and trade with overseas.

In the opposing city-state of Sparta, life was very different. There, the population was divided into two categories: the ruling Spartans and their slave population, the Helots. All Spartan boys were taken from their parents at six years old to be trained to be soldiers for the state. Life was tough, but the Spartan army was the most feared fighting force in all of Greece.

Women had little say in the way any state was run. For the most part, they were expected to stay at home, clean, cook and look after the children. Boys would be educated if their parents were wealthy enough, but anything more than a very basic education was unusual for young girls.

City-states were often at war. All able-bodied men were expected to fight in such battles, so physical fitness was essential. There were open-air gymnasiums in all city-states, where men went to meet with friends and exercise together. Wrestling, running, javelin and discus-throwing were all favourite pastimes.

The legacy of the Greeks

The ancient Greek civilisation has had a huge influence on the world we know today. The political system called democracy[1] – which comes from the Greek words *demos* (people) and *kratia* (power) – was developed in ancient Athens.

The Romans preserved much of Greek literature for later generations. Many of our modern writers return again and again to the themes of Greek stories and poetry, finding relevance even after almost three thousand years. Look around any major city in the Western world, and you will see many buildings in the 'classical' style, with fluted[2] columns supporting the distinctive triangular pediments.[3]

Greek writers and philosophers such as Plato and Aristotle are still studied as the basic texts in philosophy classes, while the plays of

1. *A political system where every man (and, in modern times, woman) is able to vote.*
2. *Having vertical grooves.*
3. *Shallow triangualr gable supported on columns.*

dramatists Euripides, Sophocles, and Aristophanes are staged in modern theatres. Technologically, the Greeks weren't as advanced as the Romans who finally dominated them, but we still have engineering and irrigation inventions to thank them for, plus developments in astronomy and urban planning.

We owe much of the English language to the Greeks as well. Some say it would be almost impossible to hold a conversation in English without using words that were used by the Greeks.

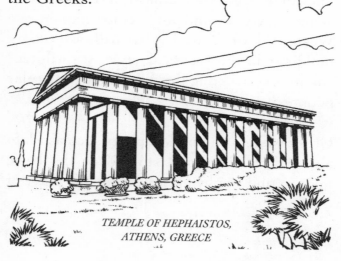

TEMPLE OF HEPHAISTOS, ATHENS, GREECE

An introduction to Greek mythology

Long before we achieved a scientific understanding of the how the natural world works, we often sought explanations that involved supernatural powers. 'Mythology' is the name given to the stories that began to be written down after the Dark Ages. They are a messy, sometimes contradictory, collection of tales that refer to the origins of the world and a time when Gods still intervened in the lives of men and women. Some are legends, in that they refer to voyages or wars that may have really existed. For instance, archaeologists have found ruins that are dated to the periods of history described in some of the myths. Indeed, there may be a grain of truth in many of them. If not, they can be seen as metaphors (another Greek word!) – representing another 'truth' about the natural world.

Almost all Greek myths involve their immortal Gods and the way they affected the lives of men and women. Often, the men and women themselves are distant relatives of the

Gods, or the Gods' sons, daughters, and descendants. This means that many of the characters have superhuman qualities, especially strength, or beauty. The Gods themselves are shown to be much like us – they fall in love, they have rivalries, they become jealous, greedy or angry. They take what they want and punish whoever has offended them. Having the blessing of one God or Goddess is no guarantee that one has the blessings of all.

The stories were told in the form of poems and plays, but also appear in travel guides, histories and stories about famous historical figures. Only a fraction of the original sources are available to us today, but we do have a fairly established set of material that we can draw from. This includes several long poems and a few dozen dramas.

However, it's important to remember that, just as our own stories change, Greek mythology was not static – there was rarely just one version of a story. In the early stages, poems were not written down, but passed

from generation to generation orally.[1] This might mean that a poet in one part of Greece might change a tale to suit his audience. But for a reader who isn't an academic, the myths can simply be fascinating tales of war, bravery, love, death and adventure.

There were literally hundreds of Greek Gods and demi-Gods, but the main ones were called the Olympians, after their home, Mount Olympus.

1. By word of mouth.

POSEIDON
God of the Sea, sender of earthquakes

HADES
Ruler of the Underworld

ZEUS
King of the Gods and ruler of Mount Olympus

HERA
Zeus' wife, Queen of the Gods

DEMETER
Goddess of farming and the seasons

MOUNT

APHRODITE
Goddess of love
and beauty

ARES
God of War

HEPHAESTUS
God of the forge,
a blacksmith

ARTEMIS
Goddess of hunting, of
maidens, and the moon

APOLLO
God of music, prophecy,
and archery

ATHENA
Goddess of
Wisdom

HERMES
Messenger of
the Gods

OLΨMPUS

CHAPTER I
THE WAR OF THE TITANS

Long before men walked the earth, and before the Gods of Olympus, led by Zeus, came to power, there existed a group of twelve gods called the Titans. They were the sons and daughters of Gaia – Goddess of the Earth – and Uranus, God of the Sky. Uranus didn't trust any of his children, especially the Cyclopes, one-eyed giants with incredible strength. He locked them in a place called Tartarus, a prison in the furthest depths of the Underworld.

But the youngest Cyclops, Cronus, overthrew his father, and ruled with his sister (who was also his wife), called Rhea. Cronus was an angry, jealous God, who guarded his throne with brutality. Each time Rhea gave birth to a new baby, he demanded that it be brought to him, and he would eat the child in front of her. This devious and horrific act ensured that no successor would ever threaten his rule.

For many years, Rhea dared not object, but one day she gave birth to a son called

Zeus. He was such a beautiful little baby that she couldn't bring herself to hand him over to her bloodthirsty husband. Instead, she wrapped a large pebble in swaddling cloths and gave this to Cronus. He was fooled and swallowed down the rock believing it to be the baby.

Rhea gave Zeus to a band of spirits called the Kouretes, who guarded him. They crashed their cymbals and other instruments whenever Cronus came near, to disguise the cries of baby Zeus. When he became an adult, Zeus visited his grandmother Gaia, who gave him a special poison to slip into Cronus' wine. However, the potion didn't kill Cronus, it just made him sick. Suddenly, up came all the contents of his stomach, including all of Zeus' brothers and sisters who had been eaten. These were the twelve Gods of Olympus.

A war began between the old Gods and the new, the Titans versus the Olympians. It was a bitter struggle. The Olympians had help from three giants, each with a hundred hands, who threw great boulders at the Titans. Zeus himself freed the Cyclopes from

Tartarus and, to show their gratitude, they fashioned special weapons for the Olympians: a trident for Poseidon, a helmet of darkness for Hades, and a thunderbolt for the King of the Gods, Zeus.

As the war raged on, the Titans were driven back. Many were killed, and others were imprisoned in Tartarus for eternity, guarded by the three giants. Those who had not fought were spared. But Atlas, the son of the Titan Iapetus, was given a special punishment: for siding with the Titans, he would have to bear the weight of the heavens upon his massive shoulders for all time. Some of the other Titans escaped, but not Cronus. He was killed by one of Zeus' thunderbolts, hurled from Mount Olympus.

After the Titans had been vanquished, the three brothers Zeus, Hades and Poseidon split the world between themselves. Hades took the Underworld, Poseidon the sea, and Zeus the heavens. Gaia, Goddess of the Earth, was left with the land, though from time to time all three brothers would interfere. From then on, the world would be ruled by the Olympians.

CHAPTER II
JASON AND THE ARGONAUTS

ing Aeson ruled Iolchus, a kingdom in Thessaly, with a fair hand. But all was not well in the land. Aeson's brother, the wicked Pelias, staged a bloody revolt, seizing the throne, imprisoning Aeson and slaying all of his children to prevent there being a successor. He even married

Aeson's pregnant queen so that there would be no threat to his power. To make sure, Pelias consulted an Oracle.[1] It gave him the prophecy:[2]

Fear only the man with one sandal.

But the gods don't look kindly on murderous men, and he had forgotten to honour one Goddess in particular: Hera, Queen of the Gods. From that day forth, she harboured bitterness towards Pelias.

When Aeson's former wife gave birth to a son soon after her imprisonment, she knew that Pelias would have the boy killed, knowing it was his brother's child. To prevent that happening, she made all of her maidservants pretend that her baby had died at birth. They stood around her chamber crying, beating their chests and tearing at their hair, as were the customs of mourning. Pelias, waiting with his dagger, was fooled.

But secretly the queen sent Jason – for that was the name she gave to the child –

1. *A place where mortals went to speak with the Gods. A priest or priestess would relay the Gods' message, often in riddles.*
2. *A prediction of the future.*

away into the mountains to be looked after by a centaur[1] called Chiron. Chiron lived in a cave away from the prying eyes of men. He brought Jason up like his own son, teaching him to read and write, to hunt wild animals in the forest, and to use plants for medicine.

When he reached manhood, Jason was eager to return to Iolchus. He thanked Chiron for the years of kindness and set off back home to reclaim his father's throne. On his way through the countryside, Jason came to a river that was almost bursting its banks. The water was brown and it carried with it bits of broken wood and large boulders. At the river's edge was an old woman. To Jason she looked about a hundred years old.

'Excuse me, kind sir,' she said. 'Will you carry me across the river?'

Chiron had brought Jason up well, so he immediately agreed, and lifted the old crone onto his back. Then he plunged into the water. It was tough going, and the water was icy cold. Jason struggled to keep his head above the water, but kept the woman safely

1. *A creature which has the body and legs of a horse, with the torso, head and arms of a man in place of its neck and head.*

on his back. When he reached the other side, Jason was annoyed to notice that he'd lost one of his sandals in the raging torrent.

At least his passenger was very grateful for his help.

'May the Gods bless you,' she said.

Jason bid her farewell and was soon at the walls of Iolchus. What he didn't know was that the old woman was not all she seemed. In fact, she was none other than the goddess Hera, enemy of Pelias.

Jason marched straight to the palace wearing his one soggy sandal and demanded to see the king. He told anyone who would listen that the throne was his.

Pelias took one look at Jason and the Oracle's words rang clear in his head:

Fear only the man with one sandal.

But he didn't want to show fear in front of his courtiers,[1] so instead of killing Jason on the spot, he asked him a question.

'What would you do if you wanted to be rid of a person, but dared not kill him yourself?'

1. *People who attend the court of the ruler.*

35

quick to answer. 'I'd send him
possible mission – to rescue the
Fleece.'

'a!' said Pelias. 'What a clever idea!'

The Golden Fleece was a magical treasure
the kingdom of Colchis.[1] Stories told of a
grove sacred to Ares, God of War, where the
Golden Fleece hung. However, it was
guarded by a fire-breathing dragon. Several
brave heroes had tried to take it, but all had
met their death in the flames from the
dragon's mouth or between its jagged teeth.

Pelias called his court together and asked
for silence.

'This boy, who claims to be the son of my
brother, wants the throne of Iolchus. I say to
him, prove you are worthy of the crown.
Fetch me the Golden Fleece and the
kingdom will be yours!'

Jason saw the trap he'd walked into, but
with the expectant eyes of the crowd upon
him, how could he refuse?

'I'll do it,' he said. 'But I'll need a boat and
a good crew.' The assembled crowd cheered.
Jason visited the best ship-builder in the city

1. *In modern-day Georgia on the Black Sea coast.*

– a man named Argus. Argus promised to build Jason a ship unlike any other. It would be faster than a dolphin, and strong enough to withstand the very worst storms the Sea God Poseidon could muster. He set to work with his team of carpenters.

News of Jason's planned voyage over the seas spread quickly through the known world. Most thought he was mad to attempt his quest, but many admired him. A small, tough bunch of men, eager for glory, slowly trickled into Iolchus, to pledge their support for Jason. Among them was Heracles – on a break from his own adventures – the strongest man in the world. The twin brothers Castor and Pollux came as well. Orpheus the musician, with his flute and lyre,[1] also offered his services. Strangely for that time, there was even a woman, Atalanta. She was well known for her skill with a bow, and her speed on foot.

When the ship – called the *Argo* after its maker – was completed, Hera asked the Goddess of Wisdom, Athena for the finishing touch. She added a prow,[2] carved in

1. *A stringed instrument.*
2. *An ornate carving on the front part of a ship.*

her own likeness to the front of the *Argo*. It had the power of speech, so that the Goddess could help to guide them on their voyage.

So, after several months, the Argonauts, as they were named, rowed out of the harbour at Iolchus on an incredible voyage of danger and discovery.

The Journey Begins

Their first stop was the island of Lemnos.[1] This place was unusual in that there wasn't a single male inhabitant anywhere. As the women of Lemnos had not worshipped the goddess Aphrodite in the proper way, she had made them all mad. Under this cloak of insanity, and in the dead of night, they had murdered all the men on the island. When they awoke the next morning, surrounded by the corpses of the slain men, the women despaired at their actions, and vowed never to neglect the Goddess again.

After so long alone, the women wanted to make the Argonauts stay with them, and the sailors themselves couldn't believe their good fortune. Under a spell of love, they stayed for over a year on Lemnos. Some even fathered children with the women living there.

Finally, it was the mighty Heracles who lost his patience. He turned to his comrades around the fire one night.

'What are we doing here? Are we mad?' he demanded.

1. *In the northern part of the Aegean Sea, between Greece and Turkey.*

'Silence,' said Telamon, another of the Argonauts. 'Life is good here.'

But Heracles stood up and, kicking sand over the fire, he grabbed Jason by the shoulders.

'You're our leader. You should know better. Have these women made you forget about your quest to find the Golden Fleece?'

His words rang true and the men threw down their wine flasks in disgust at their own foolishness. Heracles was right. This was no way for heroes to act, and they all agreed to set sail at first light.

A Tragic Misunderstanding

The crew of the *Argo* next reached the shores of the people called the Doliones, who were ruled by King Cyzicus. The king had heard of Jason's journey and treated the Argonauts kindly. They moored up in Cyzicus' harbour and he gave them a fine feast at his palace. Before night fell, the Argonauts embarked again, but soon the sky turned black and a storm descended. The *Argo* was tossed around in the ocean like a child's toy. The sails were ripped to shreds and Jason realised that if they didn't land soon, they would all be drowned. With the rowers heaving at their oars, the helmsman[1] guided the ship into a rocky cove.

Tired and exhausted, the Argonauts flopped onto the beach. But they didn't have long to rest. The glint of weapons appeared on the cliffs above them, and soon soldiers poured onto the beach. Jason and his men didn't have time to ask questions. They unsheathed their swords and defended themselves. The fight was over quickly, and

1. *The person who steers a ship.*

all of their attackers lay dead on the sand. Only at sunrise next morning did the Argonauts realise their terrible mistake. The men they'd killed weren't enemies after all – they were the Doliones. Jason went and pulled his sword out of the stomach of King Cyzicus himself.

The Argonauts were stricken with grief. They burnt the bodies of the unfortunate dead, offered prayers to the gods, and left the cursed island behind.

Two Shipmates Lost

They managed to row to Mysia on the northwest coast of Asia Minor.[1] Here they decided to rest. The ship needed repairs after the battering from the storm, and a lot of their supplies had been lost overboard or ruined by salt water. While Jason and his men went off to collect wood, Heracles' servant, a handsome young boy called Hylas, was sent with the water flasks into the hills to find a river. Hylas hadn't gone far when he came across a shady grove through which a stream flowed. He knelt by a pool of water as flat as a mirror, and took the flasks off his shoulder. As he did so, he saw something move beneath the surface of the water. Leaning closer, Hylas saw the face of a beautiful woman. He couldn't believe it. He'd never seen a real-life naiad[2] before.

As he looked, another naiad swam to her side. They were smiling at him, and beckoning with their fingers. Hylas smiled

1. *Modern-day Turkey.*
2. *A female spirit said to live in water, closely connected to rivers and springs.*

back. Then a third naiad joined them. She reached out and her arm, dripping with water, broke the pool's surface. Hylas was transfixed. Her hand stroked his cheek and hair, and slipped around the back of his neck. Then its grip tightened. Hylas struggled, but it was no use. Her other hand shot out of the pool and grabbed his arm. He screamed.

Down in the valley below, Heracles heard his servant's cries for help. He dropped his axe and sprinted up the path where Hylas had last been seen. But when he reached the edge of the pool, all that was there was a pile of water flasks. Hylas was gone.

The loss was too much for Heracles. He decided that his time with the Argonauts was over. He would return to his Labours.[1] After the *Argo* was repaired, he helped to push the boat back into the water, then wished his companions farewell.

---

1. *Heracles was a well-known Greek hero who angered Hera, wife of Zeus. He was made to undertake twelve superhuman feats, called Labours, which will be described later in this book.*

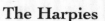
The Harpies

The other brave sailors continued their journey, and landed on the coast at Salmydessus in Thrace.[1] Here they met an elderly man called Phineus. His story was a tragic one. Granted the gift of prophecy by the God Apollo, he had angered the Gods by telling mortal men of their future. As punishment, Zeus had taken away his sight, so that Phineus would always live in complete darkness.

To make matters worse, every day Zeus would provide Phineus with a table bursting with fine food: roasted meats, sweet fruits and as much wine as he could drink. But each day, as Phineus sat down to eat, two harpies[2] would descend from the sky and steal it all way. Helpless, Phineus was left only with scraps on the ground.

The poor, ragged old man begged Jason to help him, and the hero agreed, but only on one condition.

1. *An historical region covering part of modern-day Bulgaria,*
   Turkey and Greece.
2. *Winged creatures as big as a person, with the body of a bird, but*
   the head of a woman.

'Anything!' cried Phineus.

'You have to help me on my quest,' said Jason. 'Tell me what dangers I will face and how I can overcome them.'

Phineus agreed and Jason and his men slept beneath the enchanted banquet table that night. The next morning, when the sun broke over the horizon, they smelled the delicious food above them. One of the Argonauts, called Peleus, wanted to climb out and scoff the food there and then, but Jason held him back.

'We have to wait,' he said.

When Phineus sat down to eat, a sound like a scream crossed with a screech filled the sky. The Harpies were coming. Jason leapt out from underneath the table to face them. With their black, scraggly feathers, and talons sharp as knives, the creatures flew at him. Jason stood his ground, punching them away with his shield. His men meanwhile unleashed their arrows into the sky, piercing the Harpies from all sides. The Harpies plummeted to the ground, dead. Phineus hugged Jason and thanked him.

The old man was already burying his teeth into a juicy chicken leg when Jason reminded him of their bargain.

'Now, what advice do you have for me?'

Phineus wiped his mouth.

'The only way from here to Colchis and the Golden Fleece takes you between the Clashing Rocks. Hundreds of ships have tried this route, and hundreds have been smashed to pieces when the cliffs close in. Release a dove ahead of you to test the way, and row hard, my boy. Do not stop, or death is certain.'

The Clashing Rocks

Leaving Phineus to his feast, the Argonauts put out from Salmydessus, and soon saw the narrow strait[1] ahead of them. Now, in calm weather, they couldn't see what all the fuss was about. But Jason looked closely and spied the skeleton wrecks of ships that lined the rocks on either side. As the prophet had told them, he ordered his men to the oars. Then, he took a captured dove in his hands and cast it into the air. The bird shot off between the two opposing cliff-faces. As soon as it was between them, a tremendous grinding sound filled the air, and the headlands[2] began to close in. The sea between surged as boulders the size of houses fell into the water. The daylight disappeared and the rocks crashed together. Then, as they began to open again, Jason gave his order.

'Row with all your might, men!'

Orpheus banged his drum to keep the Argonauts rowing in time, and with mighty

1. A channel of water between two landmasses.
2. The edges of the landmasses that extend into the water.

heaves, they propelled the ship between the opening rocks. When they were halfway through the straits had reached their normal width, but then the cliffs began to close in on them again.

'Faster!' bellowed Jason. 'Faster, or we'll be crushed!'

Orpheus quickened his tempo and the men pulled harder. Sweat poured from them and their muscles strained almost to breaking. The rocks were closing in, and for a moment, Jason thought they were finished. But, with the last ounce of their strength, the Argonauts prevailed and the ship burst through to the other side of the straits.

The Golden Fleece

When Jason arrived in Colchis, King Aeetes wasn't too pleased to see him. He knew very well why Jason had come, and didn't want to let him have the Golden Fleece, so he set Jason two tasks before he could claim his prize. The first was to yoke[1] a pair of oxen and plough a magical field. The second was to sow a dragon's teeth in the field.

Jason didn't think this sounded very difficult until he saw the oxen, which were taller than him, with sharp bronze hooves. To make matters worse, they breathed fire from their nostrils. Luckily for Jason, he received help from an unexpected source: King Aeetes' daughter, Medea. At the request of Hera, the Goddess Aphrodite had sent her son Eros[2] to enchant the princess, causing Medea to fall in love with Jason. Medea made a magical ointment for Jason to smear over his body, to protect him from the oxen's fiery breath.

1. *Fasten to a harness.*
2. *The God of Love.*

With great difficulty, Jason managed to get close enough to slip the harness over the beasts' heads. Once they were yoked, he guided them across King Aeetes' fields, ploughing the earth as they went. The first task was complete.

Taking the sack of dragon's teeth, Jason scattered them into the furrows like seeds. Almost as soon as the first tooth hit the ground, a sword broke through the earth. Then another. And another. Slowly, the ground erupted with a whole army of warriors wildly swinging their weapons. Jason didn't know what to do. He couldn't face so many men single-handedly. Again, Medea was on hand to help. She told Jason to throw a boulder amongst the army. He did as she said. The stone sent the warriors into confusion. They began to attack each other, not knowing where the rock had come from. Jason watched as they killed one another, leaving the field heaped with dead bodies.

Having fulfilled the king's tasks, Jason set off that night to the Grove of Ares. As he approached, he saw the gleaming Golden Fleece hanging on the branches of a dead

tree. Beneath it, coiled around the base of the trunk, was the dragon. As soon as it smelled Jason approaching, it lifted up its massive head and opened it jaws. Jason was ready, though. He reached into his sack and pulled out a piece of meat. It was drugged with a sleeping potion that Medea had prepared for him.

As the dragon lumbered towards him, Jason threw the meat into its mouth, then retreated behind a boulder to watch. The monster chewed on the morsel greedily and swallowed. For a few seconds, it looked content enough, but then its head began to sway and its eyelids drifted half-closed. With a mighty crash it collapsed beneath its tree.

Jason didn't hesitate. He climbed over the scaly body and pulled the Fleece down from the branches. It was so heavy that he struggled to lift it, but with the treasure on his back he staggered back to the *Argo* and its crew along with Medea.

King Aeetes tried to chase Jason down, but Medea betrayed him yet again. She had taken her own brother, Aspyrtus, hostage. In a moment of wickedness, she chopped him into pieces and threw his body into the sea. When the dismembered corpse washed up on the shore, King Aeetes couldn't go on. He wept for his poor son, and called out his curses to the Gods.

Talos, Giant of Bronze

One God must have heard the king's lament, because the *Argo*'s journey back to Iolchus was just as dangerous as the voyage out. The ship was blown off course towards the island of Crete. There lived a bronze-coloured giant by the name of Talos. As the Argonauts approached he picked up massive boulders and hurled them at the ship. There was no way to pass him.

But Jason was not going to be defeated so close to home. He reasoned that the giant must have a weakness. While the *Argo* sat off-shore, he took a rowing boat and landed out of sight on the island. With a small band of men, he sneaked up on Talos from behind and saw what he was looking for. On the giant's ankle there was a bronze nail about one foot long. Jason and his men crept onto the beach while Talos was still throwing rocks out to sea. They hurled a rope, lassoing it around the end of the nail. Then they heaved with all their might at the other end.

When Talos looked down it was too late. The nail popped out, and straight away the giant's dark green blood began to pour out into the sand. Talos bellowed in anger, making the cliffs rumble. He fell to one knee, trying to staunch the flow of blood with his hand, but the blood gushed out between his fingers. Then his whole body began to topple forwards. Jason and his men ran out of the way as fast as their legs could carry them as the giant thudded to the ground. Their final obstacle was out of the way.

When the *Argo* finally arrived back at the harbour in Iolchus, many years after it had departed, crowds gathered to witness the spectacle. Jason disembarked and proudly carried the Fleece up the palace steps. King Pelias was by now an old man, but his lust for power was the same as ever. He offered to give Jason a banquet of honour, but secretly he was already planning revenge. He learned that Medea was a powerful sorcerer and ordered his daughters to visit her to request a potion that would make him young again so he could fight Jason.

Medea told the girls that there was one way, and one way only, to bring back their father's youth. She told them of the ingredients of a potion that would restore life to weary limbs. They would have to chop up their father's body and place the pieces in a cauldron along with the potion. He would then be reborn as a twenty-year-old man.

As the banquet was being made ready, Pelias' daughters entered his chamber with sharpened knives. He saw them coming and asked what they were doing.

'We're going to make you young again!' said the first, as she plunged her dagger in.

'Tomorrow you will be a different man,' said another, and she did the same.

And so Pelias met his end at his daughters' hands. As they put the pieces of his corpse in the cauldron Medea appeared at their side. She, of course, had been lying all along. Pelias wouldn't be coming back at all!

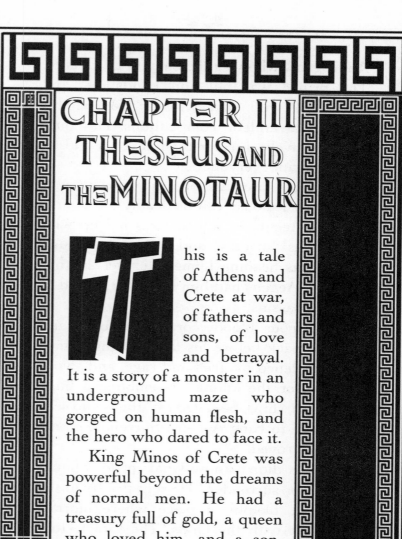

CHAPTER III
THESEUS AND THE MINOTAUR

This is a tale of Athens and Crete at war, of fathers and sons, of love and betrayal. It is a story of a monster in an underground maze who gorged on human flesh, and the hero who dared to face it.

King Minos of Crete was powerful beyond the dreams of normal men. He had a treasury full of gold, a queen who loved him, and a son,

Androgeus, who was the envy of all Greece. The prince was tall and handsome, and garlanded[1] with olive wreaths from all his victories at athletic competitions. He could throw a javelin further than anyone, and he could outrun everyone.

But such prowess breeds jealousy. And sometimes jealousy can be deadly.

King Aegeus of Athens was fed up with Androgeus' success, and when the young prince was heading home after yet another triumph, Aegeus had him killed by a band of armed assassins.

Androgeus' bloody corpse was found and brought back before his father. King Minos was maddened by grief and rage, and swore revenge for the killing. Assembling a huge fleet of warships, he sailed to Athens and sent a message to King Aegeus: Surrender to me or be destroyed.

Aegeus didn't know what to do. Should he fight, or surrender? He sent priests to the Oracle at Delphi, a place where mortals could talk with the Gods. The Oracle told him that to save his city he must obey King

1. Decorated with rings of leaves or flowers.

Minos' every command. So that is what he did. He told King Minos that he would agree to any terms he set forth. Little did he know the terrible thoughts in his enemy's mind.

Minos' demand was simple.

'Every seven years I'll come to Athens, and I will choose nine young men and nine young maidens of your city.'

'What for?' asked Aegeus.

Minos grinned. 'They will be fed to the Minotaur.'

Aegeus was horrified. All of Athens had heard of the Minotaur, but he had never believed the myth was true. It was rumoured that Minos' wife, Queen Pasiphae, had been bewitched by a sacred bull,[1] and that she had preferred to spend time with the animal rather than with her husband. To make this possible, she had enlisted the help of the most famous craftsman in Greece – a man called Daedalus. He had built for her a model of a cow that she could hide inside.

---

1. The bull had originally been given as a gift from Poseidon to
   Minos, to prove that he was the rightful king above his brothers.
   The only condition had been that Minos had to sacrifice the bull
   to the God afterwards. He hadn't, preferring to keep it. So
   Poseidon made Pasiphae fall in love with the creature.

When Pasiphae fell pregnant, Minos was very excited and told all his kingdom the good news. But on the day of the birth, his joy turned to horror. The baby was horribly deformed, with the body of a human, but the head of a bull. Eventually Minos found out the truth about the sacred bull and Daedalus' cow contraption. Through some terrible bewitchment, his wife had borne a child to the animal, and not to him.

Minos wanted to kill the child, but Pasiphae prevented him. They made a compromise: they would build a special home for the creature, underneath the King's palace. The Minotaur could live there, away from the public gaze. But how could they make sure the monster never escaped? Daedalus, wanting to make amends, suggested he build a maze which defied escape. Minos ordered it to be so.

And so, every seven years, the angry king would sail to Athens in a black-sailed boat and take away nine young men and nine young women of Minos' choosing. They would be sent into the dark recesses of the Minotaur's Labyrinth, the walls dripping

with slime, until they met their end between its massive jaws. 'A fitting price for the life of my son', thought King Minos.

But the burden weighed heavily on King Aegeus of Athens. Each time the tribute was due, he made sacrifices to the Gods and prayed for them to put an end to his torment. One day, his prayers were answered, but not in the way he expected.

A man called Theseus came to Aegeus' palace, having travelled from far away. All of Athens had heard of Theseus. He was known far and wide for his heroic deeds and great strength. What Aegeus didn't know was that Theseus was actually his son!

Many years before, when Aegeus was a young man, he had visited the kingdom of Pittheus and fallen in love with the king's beautiful daughter, Aethra. When the time came for Aegeus to return to Athens, Aethra told him she was pregnant, and that the Gods had told her the child would be a boy. Aegeus wanted to stay, but she wouldn't let him.

'You have a kingdom to rule. Upon adulthood, I'll send him to Athens.' she said.

Aegeus was sad to leave, but, as a gift, he left a sword beneath a huge boulder.

'When my son can lift the boulder, he will be ready', he said.

So Aethra gave birth alone. The child was a boy, as the Gods had foreseen. She named him Theseus.

Of course, Aegeus knew none of this, and when the hero arrived on his doorstep, his wife, a woman named Medea,[1] was suspicious of their visitor.

'He's come to take your throne,' she warned. 'Let me poison him.'

Old Aegeus loved Medea and was easily persuaded, so he let his queen mix poison in their visitor's wine. Theseus, wearied from

1. *The same Medea who helped Jason to steal the Golden Fleece!*

his long journey, lifted the cup to his lips. The story could have ended there, had Aegeus not noticed the jewelled hilt of Theseus' sword – the same one he had left under the boulder so many years before. He knocked the cup from Theseus' hand. Son and father had found each other at last. Theseus told how he had been led to a boulder by his mother on his eighteenth birthday, and had found the sword beneath. His mother, Aethra, had told him to seek his father in Athens.

Medea hated the arrival of her new stepson. No more would her son Medus be heir to the throne when her husband died. She tried to turn Aegeus against Theseus, but only succeeded in making him angry. In a fit of temper, he threw her out of his palace.

Theseus was delighted to have found his father, but his joy turned to despair when he saw the terrible state of the kingdom. It was almost time for the next sacrifice to the Minotaur. King Minos' punishment hung over the people like a dark, foreboding cloud. Each of them asked themselves who would be next for the Minotaur.

News of Theseus spread to the ears of King Minos. And so, when he arrived at Athens in his ship to choose his victims, one name was at the top of his list – Theseus. Aegeus begged him to reconsider. How could he take his only son? But Minos remained as hard as stone.

'A son for a son, fair is fair.' he said, refusing to budge.

Theseus was never a man to pass up a challenge, and bravely came forward. And so, leaving his father in tears, he climbed in Minos' boat. His father had just one wish.

'If you come home, my son, fly a white sail. That will tell me you are safe.'

Theseus was so keen to get going, he didn't listen to his father's words.

When King Minos' boat arrived in Crete, the people were gathered on the harbour to celebrate. Amongst them was a woman who was more beautiful than any Theseus had ever seen. He saw desire in her green eyes and he knew that it was love at first sight. He asked a soldier at the harbour who she was, the girl with the brown ringlets and a smile like roses.

'Oh, that's Princess Ariadne. She's King Minos' only child now.'

'I should like to meet her,' said Theseus.

The soldier laughed. 'No chance – you're going into the Labyrinth tomorrow.'

That night, when Theseus was locked up in the palace, he heard a soft step outside his door and a clunk as the heavy beam was lifted. To his surprise, his visitor was Ariadne. The couple whispered their love for one another. She told him that she hated her father and couldn't let him send Theseus into the Minotaur's lair. Theseus told her he couldn't leave his countrymen and women alone to such an awful fate. He asked if she would help him kill the Minotaur.

Ariadne said she'd do anything she could, but even if Theseus could slay the beast, there was no way to get out of the maze. It was the designer of the maze, Daedalus, who came up with an answer. He told Ariadne to give Theseus a ball of thread, and tell him to tie it to the doorpost as he entered.

It was close to midnight when Theseus reached the doorway to the Labyrinth near the Palace gardens. He followed Ariadne's

instructions, tying one end of the thread to the doorpost. The princess watched nervously as he disappeared into the gloomy darkness below.

As Theseus crept along the winding tunnels, he felt the hair on his neck rise with fear. There were no lights in the Labyrinth, and every noise – the dripping of water, the crunching of bones beneath his feet – seemed magnified. With one hand he felt along the cold rock of the winding tunnel walls. His other hand gripped the handle of his sword. He walked for what seemed like hours, growing used to the sound of his thudding heart.

Then he heard another noise – a heavy, rasping breath up ahead. Theseus strained his eyes, but could see nothing. The breathing grew closer, and turned into a low growl. Theseus lifted his sword. Suddenly there was a crashing sound coming towards him. Theseus waited until he was sure, then brought his blade down in one fierce movement. Something huge smashed into him, bellowing in pain, and Theseus sprawled onto the floor. There was silence.

He felt into the darkness until his fingers came to rest on something cold and smooth. From its shape, Theseus knew it was a horn. He then caught hold of another horn. Both were mounted on a furred head the size of a barrel. Its eyes were closed. Its body lay a few feet away. Theseus had severed the Minotaur's head.

Flushed with victory, Theseus followed the thread back out of the Labyrinth, dragging the head of the beast with him. The thin light of dawn was up when he emerged. Ariadne screamed in shock when she saw what he had brought with him, then threw her arms around her hero.

Leaving the Minotaur's head at the entrance to the Labyrinth, Theseus and Ariadne crept into the palace to release the other prisoners. Then they dashed to the harbour, where Minos' boat was still moored. They pulled up the anchor and set sail for Athens.

Minos was furious when his guards discovered what had happened. He hurried down to the harbour to chase the escaped prisoners, but found his entire fleet had been

sunk by Theseus. All he could do was watch as the hero of Athens sailed away in his boat with his daughter.

A storm at sea forced Theseus to moor up at the island of Naxos. That night, by a fire on the beach, he told Ariadne that he was going to make her queen of Athens, and she pledged her love for eternity. It took her by surprise, then, when she awoke the next morning to find Theseus, and the other Athenians, missing. No-one knows why he left her behind – perhaps he had been lying to her all along, or maybe some mischievous God bewitched his senses.

One thing is for sure, Theseus paid the price. As he approached the harbour at Athens, he forgot his father's request to fly a white sail on his mast. Aegeus watched from a clifftop above the city, and saw a black-sailed boat approaching. It could only mean one thing – his dearest son was dead. Tormented by despair, he threw himself onto the rocks below. Theseus and his crew reached Athens to find the city in mourning.

And what of Ariadne? Well, she soon grew tired of filling the sea with her tears and lay down to rest. It so happened that Naxos was the home of Dionysus, God of Merriment. He took pity on Ariadne, and soon made her his wife. When she died, many years later, he took her wedding crown and placed it up in the stars to honour her for all eternity.

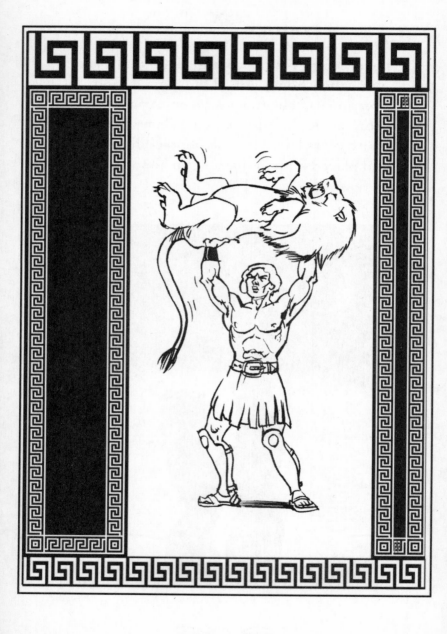

CHAPTER IV
THE TWELVE LABOURS OF HERACLES

The Gods have long memories, and what may pass for many years in our world is but a blink of the eye to them. So when her husband Zeus had a child with a mortal woman called Alcmene, the Goddess Hera didn't strike straight away. Instead she waited until the child was a man with his own family and then she took revenge. She cast a fit of madness onto the man, called Heracles, which sent him into a frenzy of violence. He knew nothing of what was happening until he woke up to see around him the dead bodies of his wife and children.

Heracles' shame was too much for him to bear. He had lost all that he held dear, and couldn't face the world. Eventually it was his friend Theseus who told him to pull himself together and ask for the Gods' forgiveness. So Heracles visited the Oracle of Delphi and asked what he could do to make up for his terrible deed. The priest's answer was that he should go to King Eurystheus of Tiryns and perform twelve tasks for him.

Heracles went straight to the King's court and threw himself at his feet. Eurystheus had hated Heracles for many years,[1] and saw his chance to make Heracles' life a misery. So he set the most impossible labours he could think of. First was to kill the Lion of Nemea, a fearsome beast that had eaten farm animals and killed people. Its skin was so thick that

1. *Both Eurystheus and Heracles were grandchildren of the hero Perseus. Eurystheus was also a champion of the Goddess Hera, who despised Heracles.*

no weapon could penetrate it, but Heracles strangled the beast with his bare hands. He skinned the lion and wore its fur as a cloak.

Next Eurystheus sent Heracles to the lake of Lerna, to slay the creature that lurked in the water. It was a Hydra, a sea serpent with seven heads. Heracles took a sickle and tried to cut off each head, but every time he chopped off one head, two more grew back. Help came from Heracles' nephew, Iolas, who came up with a solution. Iolas took a firebrand[1] and, each time Heracles sliced off a head, he placed the flame against the

---

1. *A tight bundle of sticks, set alight at one end so that it burns slowly.*

bleeding stump to prevent another head growing. By doing this, Heracles was able to defeat the Hydra and its body sank beneath the water for ever.

By this stage, King Eurystheus was angry. He decided that Heracles was too good at killing creatures, so he asked him to catch the next one alive. The Ceryneian Hind was a deer sacred to the Goddess Artemis. Men said it could run faster than an arrow and could fly. Heracles chased the Hind for a full year until he finally caught it when it stopped for a drink by a stream.

Eurystheus didn't know what to do next, so he sent Heracles on his most dangerous mission yet – to capture the massive, angry boar that lived on Mount Erymanthos. Heracles asked for advice from the centaur Chiron, who told him that the best way to catch the creature was to drive it up the mountain into deep snow. And so Heracles chased the boar up the slope, threw a huge net over its back, and dragged the beast back to the castle. King Eurystheus almost fell off his throne when he saw the boar's red eyes and huge yellow tusks.

The king then ordered Heracles to carry out a filthy task – to clean the stables of King Augeas of Elis in a single day. Augeas kept hundreds of smelly cattle there and hadn't changed the straw or even taken a broom to the stable floor for twenty years. Again, it was Heracles' clever nephew Iolas who devised a plan. Together they climbed into the nearby valley, where a wide river flowed. Heracles used his great strength to roll boulders into the river's path. In this way, they managed to divert the river towards the king's stables. Iolas opened the stable doors and the torrent of water blasted through, taking all the debris and filth with it.

For his next task, Eurystheus sent Heracles to the marsh of Stymphalos. There lived a flock of menacing birds. With brass claws and wings of bronze, they were the favourite pets of Ares, the God of War. The birds terrorised the local people. Their droppings poisoned the rivers and crops. But worst of all, the birds carried off cattle and even children.

Heracles' first problem was that the birds would not come out and fight – they knew of

his reputation and stayed safely in their nests high up in the trees. So Heracles visited Hephaestus, the God sacred to blacksmiths, to ask for his help. Hephaestus fashioned a set of bronze clappers[1] for the hero, and when he banged these together, the birds couldn't help but stir from their perches because of the noise. Heracles dealt with them quickly, shooting them out of the sky with his arrows.

On Eurystheus' orders, Heracles went next to Crete, where King Minos was ruler. There, a fearless bull was roaming the fields, trampling anyone who came near. Heracles was showing off by this stage, so instead of killing the Cretan Bull, he tackled it with his bare hands, and carried it alive all the way back to King Eurystheus. At first, the king wanted to sacrifice the creature to the Goddess Hera, but she refused. There was no way she would consider accepting such an honour from Heracles, whom she despised. The bull was eventually freed into the plains of Marathon, where it roamed happily until

1. *A musical instrument, made up of two pieces of wood or metal that strike each other to make a loud sound.*

the hero known as Theseus captured it many years later.[1]

King Eurystheus had long hated the king of the Bistonian race, a giant called Diomedes. This king was feared throughout the world because he kept four man-eating horses. Eurystheus ordered Heracles to tame the horses, but this task would not be so easy. The mares had teeth of iron, which could tear a person to pieces. Heracles knew that he wouldn't be able to handle the horses and Diomedes and the Bistones on his own, so he took a friend called Abderus with him.

Under the cover of darkness, Heracles crept ashore into the stables of Diomedes and bound the horses to a chariot. But as he drove them out of the stables, the pounding of their hooves and angry whinnying awoke the king, who ordered the Bistones to attack.

Heracles left Abderus with the horses, while he held off the soldiers, slaying hundreds of them. But when he got back to his ship, where the horses were waiting, Abderus was nowhere to be seen. Heracles discovered a piece of his friend's bloody

1. *This bull is not to be confused with the Minotaur, which was half-man, half-bull.*

clothing between one of the horse's teeth. Not for the first time, Heracles lost his temper. In a rage he fought his way into Diomedes' palace and seized the giant.

'Your horses will eat well today!' he said, and with that he threw the king to his own beasts. After that, they would never eat human flesh again.

For his ninth labour, King Eurystheus sent our hero to the land of the warrior women called the Amazons. This powerful army of women on horseback was ruled by Queen Hippolyta, daughter of Ares, God of war. Eurystheus wanted Hippolyta's girdle[1] for his daughter. When Heracles' boat reached the shore, Hippolyta fell in love with him at once, and offered him the girdle of her own free will. They feasted together that night.

Finishing the task would have been easy if it hadn't been for the meddling of the goddess Hera. As Heracles and Hippolyta slept by the fireside, Hera came down from Olympus disguised as an Amazon. She told all the other women that Heracles had come

1. *A sort of belt encircling a woman's waist.*

to kidnap their queen, and a battle began. Heracles awoke to find himself and his men being attacked, and had no choice but to fight back. In the skirmish, he let loose an arrow that struck the unlucky Hippolyta in the chest. Filled with grief, Heracles returned home. This was the second woman he had killed, and all because Hera loathed him so.

Heracles' tenth mission had him facing up to Geryon, a giant with a difference, who lived far away in the western seas. Though Geryon had only one body, he had six arms, six legs and three heads! Eurystheus' task was to capture the famous cattle that Geryon guarded with the help of his two-headed hound called Orthrus. Heracles simply clubbed Orthrus over the head, and the dog was no more.

Geryon was a trickier opponent. He carried three shields and three spears, and each of his heads was covered by a thick helmet. Heracles had a secret weapon, though. Since killing the Lernaean Hydra, he had kept a vial[1] of its poisonous blood.

1. *A small glass bottle.*

He dipped an arrow in this toxic substance and fired it straight into Geryon's heart. Thrashing his arms and legs, and wailing in anger, the giant died. Heracles travelled home over the sea in a special golden bowl given to him by the Sun-God Helios, which was big enough to fit the cattle in as well.

Eurystheus wasn't particularly pleased to see Heracles again, so this time he set him a task that he knew he couldn't complete: to fetch the sacred apples from the Garden of the Hesperides. These were three nymphs[1] who tended the garden for the goddess Hera.

Heracles knew that if he even tried to get into the orchard, Hera would not let him live, so he decided on a roundabout route. He needed the help of Atlas, the Titan who held the heavens on his shoulders. He was the father of the Hesperides, so he'd be able to get into the garden without any trouble. But Heracles had no idea where to find him. So first he went to see Prometheus, the Titan who had been chained to a rock by Zeus for stealing the gift of fire from the Gods and giving it to mortals. Every day Prometheus'

1. *A nymph is a lesser female immortal. Nymphs often inhabited*
   places such as forests, streams and caves.

liver was torn out by an eagle, only to grow back overnight.

Heracles promised to release Prometheus if he told him where to find Atlas. Prometheus agreed straight away, and as soon as Heracles had broken his chains, he led the hero to where Atlas was holding up the heavens. The Titan had been there for thousands of years, so when Heracles asked him to fetch the golden apples, he had only one condition.

'If you hold up the heavens for a little while, I'll do anything you ask.'

Heracles agreed, and with great care, Atlas rolled the heavens onto the hero's shoulders. Atlas went off to Hera's garden to get the apples. Heracles waited and waited, until finally Atlas returned.

'Right then,' he said. 'Let's swap back.'

Atlas wasn't so keen. He had forgotten how good it felt without such a weight on his shoulders, so he refused. Heracles managed to control his temper.

'Very well,' he said. 'If I must hold up the heavens, at least let me straighten my tunic first. Can you hold it just for a second?'

Atlas agreed, but as soon as he'd taken the heavens back again, Heracles took the apples and walked off. The Titan was left to rue his own stupidity.

Heracles burst into Eurystheus' court, juggling the apples in triumph, but the king only gave a cruel smile.

'Well, done, Heracles,' he said. 'But it's the final labour that will be the death of you.'

He ordered Heracles to bring him Cerberus, the guard dog of the underworld. Even Heracles gulped at this one. Cerberus was no ordinary mutt: he was a hound from hell with three heads and a coat bristling with poisonous snakes. But, undaunted, Heracles sharpened his sword, and went to Taenarum, a lake that served as the gate to the Underworld.

He descended through the shadows into the depths of the earth, until finally he came to the throne of Hades, God of the Underworld. He explained his mission, and asked to be allowed to take the beast back with him. Hades agreed, but on the condition that Heracles subdued Cerberus using only his brute strength.

The fight lasted over a day as man and beast rolled around on the ground, each one struggling desperately to gain an advantage over the other. Eventually, Heracles managed to wrestle Cerberus into submission and dragged him all the way back to King Eurystheus.

When the king saw Cerberus' snarling, slavering jaws, he jumped right inside an empty pithos.[1] Peeping over the top, he said he'd had enough. He begged the hero to return the dog to the Underworld, and never to come back again.

Heracles was only too happy to obey. His mission was finally over, and he had paid the price for his family's death.

1. A large, wide-mouthed wine-jar.

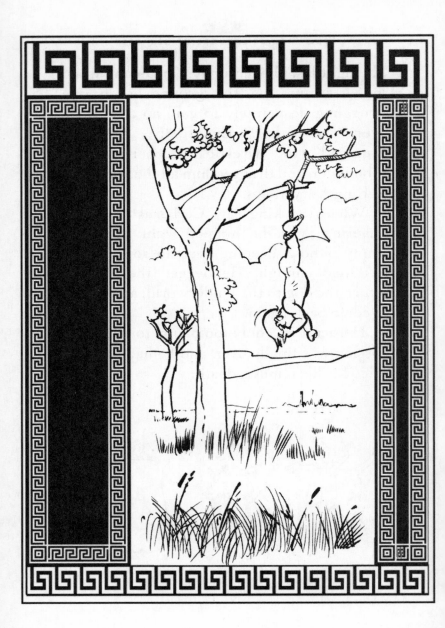

CHAPTER V
THE CURSE
OF THEBES

Many of the famous myths are all about mortals trying to escape their fate, and the story of Oedipus and the curse of Thebes is no exception. An Oracle had told King Laius of Thebes that he would be killed by his son, so when his wife Jocasta gave birth to a boy, with regret he passed the baby on to a shepherd and asked him to kill the child in the mountains. The shepherd couldn't bear to carry out the murder himself, so he tied the baby's feet together with twine and hung him from the branch of a tree.

That would have been the end of things, if a passing peasant hadn't found the child, wailing and shivering in the cold. He took pity and cut the boy down. The peasant, too poor and weak to care for the baby himself, continued on to his destination, a kingdom called Corinth, where he left the baby at the palace gates.

It so happened that Polybus, King of Corinth, had no child of his own, so he adopted the boy, and called him Oedipus.[1] Oedipus grew up to be a fine young man, and never knew that he wasn't really a prince of Corinth. His life was happy enough until he himself visited an Oracle on his twentieth birthday. The priest there told him that he would kill his father and marry his mother.

The prophecy hit Oedipus like a thunderbolt. He was terrified that it might come true. As he loved his father and mother

1. *The name means 'swollen foot' in Greek (from 'oidein', to swell and 'pous', foot).*

dearly, he decided the only way to avoid such a terrible fate was to leave Corinth immediately, and to go into hiding. So, taking only a sack of clothes and some food, he set out north, in the middle of the night.

It was on the road to Thebes, the next day, that Oedipus came across an older man in a chariot. Instead of letting him pass, the charioteer drove straight at him, shouting for Oedipus to move out of the way. Oedipus was a proud young man, a prince, no less, and he wasn't used to being ordered about like a common peasant. Just as the chariot was about to run him over, he grabbed a fence post and threw it at the chariot driver.

The post hit the man's head and killed him instantly. Little did he know that he had just killed his real father, Laius, the King of Thebes. He buried the body by the side of the road and carried on towards Thebes.

He found the city devastated by a monster called the Sphinx, a winged lion with the head of a woman. This terrifying creature was eating the crops in the fields, and drinking the rivers dry. The only way she could be killed, it was said, was if someone from Thebes could solve her riddle. Many had tried already, but all had failed. The punishment for getting the answer wrong was to die between her massive jaws.

The queen of Thebes, Jocasta, told Oedipus that her husband himself had gone to take on the riddle, but since he had not returned, she assumed he, too, was dead. She didn't know that she was actually talking to her husband's murderer.

Oedipus was a brave man, and thought himself clever, so he agreed to take up the Sphinx's challenge. He travelled out to the cave where the beast lived and presented himself before it:

'I, Oedipus, am here to solve your riddle!'

'Very well,' said the Sphinx. 'Tell me this: what goes on all fours in the morning, on two legs in the afternoon, and on three legs in the evening?'

Oedipus pondered on the puzzle for a few seconds, and just as the Sphinx was about to spring forward and devour him, he spoke:

'Man is the answer, for he is born a baby and crawls on the ground. As an adult he learns to walk on two feet. And when he is old, in the evening of his life, he walks with a cane, giving him three legs.'

As he watched, the Sphinx gave a scream and was consumed in a ball of white-hot flames. The curse was lifted and Oedipus immediately returned to Thebes. There he was applauded as a saviour and hero. Jocasta, in her gratitude, married him and made Oedipus king.

Together, king and queen ruled happily for many years, having four children: twin boys called Eteocles and Polynices, and two daughters, Antigone and Ismene.

Soon after their births, a terrible plague began to affect the city of Thebes, killing

hundreds of men, women and children. Despite the work of the best physicians and people praying to the gods day and night, the deaths continued. Finally Oedipus consulted a soothsayer[1] called Tiresias.

'Tell me what I should do to stop this pestilence,' he begged.

'Do not look for the cause,' warned Tiresias. 'It will only do you harm.'

But Oedipus insisted. He called forth anyone in Greece to tell him why Thebes was so afflicted. Eventually an elderly shepherd came forward.

'I can tell you, king of Thebes,' he said. 'But you will not like the truth.'

Oedipus was impatient and threatened to have the man whipped if he didn't speak up.

'Very well,' said the shepherd. 'You are not the son of Polybus, as you believe. Your father was Laius, the man whom you killed.'

At first, Oedipus didn't believe him. But the shepherd explained that it was he who had taken the young Oedipus to the mountains and hung him from the branch. He had seen a traveller take the baby away.

1. *Someone who tells the future.*

Oedipus dropped to his knees. The Oracle's prophecy had come true. He had killed his father. A worse thought dawned through his despair: 'I've married my mother. I've had children by her!'

And word of this spread quickly. Shortly after, from behind him in his palace, Oedipus heard a scream. The doors were suddenly flung open, and a maidservant burst through them. Tears rolled down her eyes as she broke the terrible news. 'Jocasta, your wife, your mother, is dead! She has killed herself with your sword!'

Oedipus, in the horror of what he had done, took his dagger and poked out his own eyes. Never again did he wish to look upon the world.

CHAPTER VI
PERSEUS
AND MEDUSA

King Acrisius of Argos had been told by an Oracle that he would die at the hands of his grandson. Since he only had one child, a woman called Danae, he locked her up in a tower where she could never meet a husband and have children. But once the Gods had decided on something, there was no point trying to avoid fate. Zeus came down to Danae in the form of a shower of rain, and she fell pregnant. When the child a boy, was born, Danae named him Perseus.

King Acrisius was worried, but he didn't dare kill baby Perseus, in case it angered Zeus. So he did the next best thing. He ordered his soldiers to put Danae and her child into a large chest and to throw them into the sea. If they died, Acrisius reasoned, he could blame Zeus' brother, Poseidon, the God who ruled the oceans.

Zeus spoke with Poseidon and asked him to keep the chest safe, so Poseidon made sure the waves were small, and eventually the chest washed up on the island of Seriphos.[1] It was found by a fisherman called Dictys, who happened to be the brother of Polydectes, the king of Seriphos.

As soon as the king set eyes upon Danae he wanted to make her his queen, so he separated mother and child. He took Danae to live with him in the palace, and Perseus grew up with Dictys, learning how to be a fisherman. But Polydectes was always

1. *Known as Serifos in modern times – one of the islands called the Cyclades in the Aegean Sea to the east of modern Greece.*

worried that Perseus might come to rescue his mother, so he devised a plan to get rid of her son once and for all.

Polydectes pretended he was going to marry a woman called Hippodamia, who was very fond of horses. So he asked each of the most important lords in his kingdom, and also Perseus, to give him a horse as a wedding gift. Of course, he was well aware that Perseus didn't have the money to buy him a horse, so the boy visited Polydectes' palace and fell right into the king's trap.

'I can't give you a horse,' he said, 'but whatever else you want, I'll bring.'

Polydectes gave a wicked smile.

'Then bring me the head of Medusa,' he said for all his court to hear.

Perseus realised his error. Medusa was one of the three sisters known as the Gorgons. Once a beautiful woman, she had been transformed into a hideous monster by the Goddess Athena. Now she had the face of an old woman, and her hair was a writhing mass of vipers. It was said that just to look into her terrifying eyes would turn a man to stone on the spot.

Perseus had made a promise to the king and for many days he didn't know what to do. He couldn't even find Medusa, let alone kill her. Help came, though, in the form of the Gods Hermes and Athena. They gave him three gifts. The first gift was a curved adamantine[1] sword and the second was a shield so polished that he could see himself in its surface. These would help him in his quest to kill the Gorgon. The last gift was a pair of special sandals like those that Hermes wore. They had little wings on the sides that would allow Perseus to fly through the air like a bird.

'But how can I find Medusa?' he asked.

'You must seek the answer from her cousins, the Grey Witches,' said Athena.

Perseus thanked them and, using the winged sandals, he took to the skies.

The Grey Witches were three old crones who lived in a dank cave. All three were blind, but they had a single seeing eye that they passed between them. Perseus landed at the cave entrance and saw their bent, filthy forms crouching by a fire inside.

---

1. *A legendary stone of incredible strength, like a diamond.*

The witches all turned towards him at the sound of his footsteps. The witch with the eyeball squinted and said:

'It's a young man!'

'Tell me where I can find Medusa!' Perseus demanded.

The witch popped out her eyeball and passed it to her neighbour.

'We won't tell you!' the second witch said. Perseus didn't have time to waste. As the second witch was passing the eye to the third, he shot forward and seized it. The three horrible hags screamed and tried to claw at him with their nails, but Perseus easily dodged their blind attacks.

'For the last time, tell me where I can find Medusa,' he said.

The Grey Witches had no choice, so they told him what he wanted to know. Perseus hurled their eyeball to the back of the cave and turned to leave. Behind him he heard the three witches scrabbling in the darkness.

Perseus travelled north to where Medusa lived in the remains of her ruined house. The first thing he noticed was all the statues in her garden – men in all shapes and sizes,

many carrying weapons. He looked closer. The sculptures looked so real! Perseus' blood ran cold, and he suddenly understood.

These were no statues. They were the petrified[1] corpses of real men!

All had looked upon the Gorgon's hideous face. Perseus shuddered and continued his journey into the empty halls of her home. Suddenly he heard something like a whisper. He hid behind the statue of another victim, and waited. The whispering was more like hissing, and it was getting closer. Perseus knew that if his eyes looked directly at Medusa's face he, too, would become just another statue in her halls.

'What can I do?' he thought. 'How can I kill her if I can't look upon her?'

The hissing was only a few feet away now. Then he thought of his shield! Holding the shield up, he could use the polished surface as a mirror. When he first caught sight of the Gorgon monster in the shield's reflection, he felt his heart go cold with fear, but at least he hadn't turned to stone. Medusa was wearing a long white gown, and seemed to

1. *Turned to stone in an instant.*

float across the floor. But her head was what held his attention most. Her hair seethed with writhing snakes, and her face was covered with thick scales. Her eyes were as red as smouldering embers. Perseus gripped the hilt of his sword and prayed for success.

'I know you're in here,' hissed Medusa. 'Look at me when I'm talking to you!'

Perseus kept his eyes on the reflection in his shield, until Medusa was almost on him, then he jumped out with his eyes closed and swung his sword. The blade cut through something, and he heard a gurgling scream cut short. When he opened his eyes, he could see the Gorgon's head toppling down the steps beside him.

Perseus dropped his prize into a sack and headed back to Seriphos. His adventures weren't over yet, however. On the way home, he was flying over the kingdom of Ethiopia, when a strange sight caught his eye. It was a beautiful young woman chained to a rock. He flew down and landed by her side.

'What are you doing here?' he asked.

The woman told him her name was Andromeda. She was to be fed to a sea

monster, because her mother had angered the Gods by boasting about her beauty. Perseus didn't believe her at first, but then he heard a roar behind him, and turned to see the gaping jaws of a giant beast emerge from the waves. He didn't have time to think.

'Close your eyes!' he said to Andromeda, and pulled Medusa's head from the sack, thrusting it towards the sea. The sea creature's eyes widened, its green scales turned to grey, and its jaws locked in place. It

had turned to solid rock! With a mighty splash, it plunged back under the water, sinking like a stone. Perseus had rid the kingdom of a menace and freed Andromeda. Later he would return and marry her, but for the time being he had more important things on his mind.

When he arrived back at Seriphos, Perseus found that King Polydectes had actually married Danae, his mother, and was keeping her prisoner in the King's palace. The king was surprised to see Perseus again, and ordered his soldiers to kill the insolent boy. However, this time the hero was ready. He took out Medusa's head again, revealing the horrible face to his enemies. All of them, Polydectes included, were rooted to the spot, as their bodies turned to stone.

With his mother freed, the story could have ended there, but the Gods still had a prophecy to fulfil, and the Gods liked nothing more than being true to their word. Perseus soon decided to compete in the athletic games in a place called Larissa.[1] It was there that he entered the discus

1. *In the northern part of modern Greece.*

competition. When it was his turn, he summoned all of his strength and launched the discus into the air. It span out of the stadium and out of sight. Perseus couldn't believe his own strength! Some spectators even said that the Gods must have been involved. They were probably right, because it was later discovered that the discus had struck and killed a man walking on the road just outside.

Of course, it was Acrisius, the king of Argos, the very man who had been warned that his death would come at the hands of his own grandson.

CHAPTER VII
THE
CALYDONIAN
BOAR HUNT

There are times when one hero isn't enough. The tale of the Calydonian Boar is one such occasion. The land of Calydon was ruled by a man called Oeneus. Half of his kingdom was covered in vineyards and he was famous for the wine he produced. Every year, King Oeneus would hold sacrifices for all the Gods, because as every Greek knows, the key to good fortune is to keep the Gods on Mount Olympus happy.

But one year, King Oeneus made a grave mistake: he forgot to honour the Goddess Artemis. In a rage, jealous of the other Gods, Artemis decided to punish Oeneus for his forgetfulness, so she let loose a giant, angry wild boar into his vineyards. The creature, as big as a cow, had bristles as sharp as knives and long yellow teeth. It soon ravaged the countryside, tearing up the thick, twining vines.

Oeneus didn't know what to do. The people of his kingdom were too scared even to step outside the city walls. So he sent out messengers all over the Greek world, asking if any man was brave enough to face up to the Boar and rid his kingdom of this terrible, destructive beast.

Greek heroes loved nothing more than a challenge, and soon men were arriving from every direction. There were dozens of them, including the sons of Gods, some of the Argonauts, Odysseus' father Laertes, and even the great Theseus from Athens. The only person not to come was Heracles who had already tackled a boar sent by the Gods and so had nothing left to prove. Even one woman turned up, which was odd in the age of heroes. Her name was Atalanta, and she was known all over the world for her speed – it was said that she ran faster than the wind. Some of the other hunters weren't happy about this; they didn't think a woman should be allowed to join them. The son of King Oeneus, a man called Meleager, led the hunting party.

Meleager had an interesting past. Three nights after his birth, three Goddesses, called the Fates, had appeared to Meleager's mother, Althaea. They told her he would live as long as she kept a special log burning in the fireplace of the family home. Of course, Althaea quickly threw the log into the flames, where it had remained ever since. To keep Meleager safe on the hunt, Althaea sent her two brothers, Toxeus and Plexippus, along to accompany him.

As the hunters entered the forest where the Boar liked to hide, they were all eager to be the one who struck the fatal blow. Some

even said that the Boar wasn't sent by the Gods, and that King Oeneus was exaggerating. One of the Argonauts, a man called Eurytion, said he would even tackle the creature with his bare hands.

Soon they were on the Boar's trail, in the depths of the forest. There was the sound of a twig cracking, and feet pounding on the ground up ahead. The men scattered, ready to throw their spears. The foliage began to move and a hunter called Peleus was the first to throw his spear. There was a scream. Parting the leaves, Peleus saw that his spear was buried in the stomach of his friend Eurytion. After this tragedy, everyone fell utterly quiet.

On they plunged between the trees, until again the Boar charged. When the hunters first laid eyes on the beast, they were frozen with fear. Anchaeus was gored[1] in the groin and died in agony. Atalanta was the first to give chase, leaping over fallen trunks and through forest streams, not once letting the Boar leave her sight. The others tried to keep up, but she was much too quick for them.

1. *Pierced with an animal's horn or tusk.*

Finally, the Boar began to tire, and Atalanta, still in pursuit, strung an arrow to her bow. She took careful aim and fired. The shaft shot through the air and buried itself in the beast's leg. The Boar roared in pain and skidded to a halt. At this moment Meleager stepped forward and drove his spear through its heart. The Boar of Calydon was dead.

The other hunters cheered and began to skin the Boar's thick hide as a prize for Meleager. They tried to lift him onto their shoulders, but he wouldn't let them.

'The prize goes to Atalanta,' he said. 'She's the one who first drew blood.'

The men cried out their disapproval.

'She's just a woman with a lucky arrow! You were the one who rid your father's kingdom of this menace.'

But Meleager was insistent. He wouldn't back down. Finally, his uncle Toxeus spoke.

'It's only because you are in love with her.'

Plexippus agreed.

'Yes, you're under the woman's spell', Plexippus agreed.

Meleager wouldn't stand for this, and killed them both with his spear still dripping

with the Boar's blood. He turned and gave the Boar's hide to Atalanta.

King Oeneus was delighted to hear his land was freed of its curse, and offered sacrifices to all of the Gods, including Artemis this time. But his wife was not so happy. When she found out what had happened to her dear brothers, she went straight to the family hearth and seized the enchanted log with a pair of tongs.

'As you killed my brothers,' she said. 'So I will bring your end.'

With that, she lifted the log from the flames. The Fates took note, and snipped the thread that measured Meleager's life. In his chamber with Atalanta, Meleager dropped down dead. King Oeneus had freed his land of the menace of the Boar but paid for it with the life of his son.

CHAPTER VIII
THE TROJAN WAR

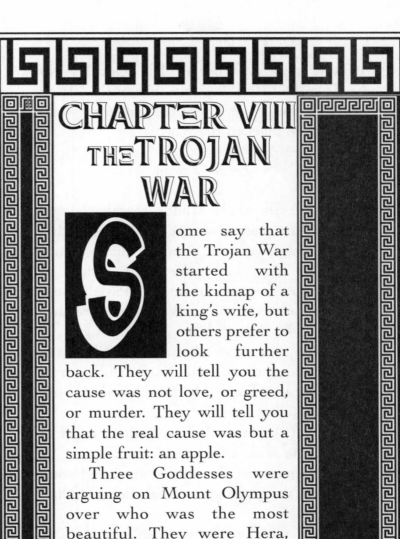

Some say that the Trojan War started with the kidnap of a king's wife, but others prefer to look further back. They will tell you the cause was not love, or greed, or murder. They will tell you that the real cause was but a simple fruit: an apple.

Three Goddesses were arguing on Mount Olympus over who was the most beautiful. They were Hera,

Athena and Aphrodite. The Goddess of Strife, called Eris, had mischievously left an apple in the grove where they liked to walk. On it were marked the words:

For the Fairest

Of course, the three Goddesses all claimed the fruit for themselves. When they couldn't decide, they went to a mortal man, Prince Paris of Troy, and asked him which of them was the most beautiful. Paris would have done better to walk away there and then, but he didn't. After much thought, he gave the apple to Aphrodite. She was delighted, and offered Paris the mortal woman of his choice. He didn't need to think very long.

'I want the most desired woman in all of Greece,' he said. 'Give me Helen.'

And there lies the seed that would soon grow into the greatest war that the world had ever seen.

Helen was the wife of King Menelaus of Sparta. People said that without a doubt she was the most beautiful woman who had ever

lived. At this time, Sparta and Troy were at peace. That summer, the Spartans were hosting a banquet for their friends from over the sea. Prince Paris was there with his older brother Hector, toasting Menelaus' generosity and drinking his wine. But when night fell, Aphrodite fulfilled her promise to Paris. She cast a spell on Helen, making her fall in love with Paris. The Trojan prince took her to his ship and sailed back to Troy.

And so, Menelaus woke the next morning to find his bed empty. It was a crime that could not go unavenged. Menelaus immediately summoned his brother, King Agamemnon of neighbouring Mycenae, to tell him what had happened. He reminded his brother of the promise they had once made to Helen's father, Tyndareus: that, should harm ever come to her, all the kings of Greece would unite to save her. Agamemnon swore to help his brother, and sent his messengers to all of the cities, telling the leaders to bring their men and their ships to the port at Aulis.

When autumn came, the troops gathered on the coast of Aulis. It was the greatest army

the world had ever seen. Thousands of ships and hundreds of thousands of men were ready to set sail towards Troy. Their secret weapon was a legendary fighter called Achilles. People believed that he was invincible because his mother, a nymph called Thetis, had taken him to the Underworld as a baby and dipped him in the waters of the River Styx.[1]

But a problem arose. While assembling by the coast, Agamemnon and some of his men went hunting. They shot a deer, and roasted it over their campfires, but as they ate, the winds dropped to nothing. Without wind the fleet could not sail.

'This is the Gods' work,' said one of the men, and he was right.

Agamemnon consulted a priest called Calchas, who told him the awful truth. The deer they had eaten was sacred to the Goddess Artemis, who was well known for her short temper. Calchas told the king that the only one way to appease Artemis was to sacrifice his own daughter, a young woman

---

1. A river that flowed in the Underworld, separating the world of the living from the world of the dead.

called Iphigenia. Agamemnon was in despair. On the one hand he had made a promise to protect Helen, and on the other hand rested the life of his dearest child. After many nights lying awake under the stars, he finally made the difficult choice. He took Iphigenia with him to overlook the fleet from a high cliff. When they reached the top, his daughter turned and saw tears in his eyes.

'Why are you crying, father?' she asked.

Agamemnon wiped his eyes and pushed his daughter off the cliff. She died on the rocks below. As her body slowly drifted out to sea, the wind began to blow. The Goddess was happy, and the fleet could sail at last.

Meanwhile, protected by their thick city walls, the Trojans weren't sure what to do. Paris was one of the many children of old King Priam. Some Trojans wanted to give Helen back, saying that it was foolish to fight over a woman. Others, who didn't like the Greeks, said that they shouldn't give in, and that they should trust their tall city walls to protect them. After all, the defences had never once been breached. They eventually decided to fight.

The war lasted for ten long years. Many battles were fought between the heroes of both armies, and even the Gods took sides. Menelaus offered to fight Paris one on to one, and the prince agreed, even though he was known to be a poor fighter. Normally he preferred to stay at a distance and use his bow and arrow, but now he was forced to meet the man he had wronged face to face. Menelaus quickly took the upper hand, but just as he was about to bury his sword in the Trojan Prince, Paris vanished into thin air. It was the work of the Goddess Aphrodite again – spiriting away her favourite. It made Menelaus angrier still.

At first Achilles barely fought at all. He was sulking in his tent because Agamemnon had stolen his Trojan slave, the beautiful Briseis. His young friend Patroclus, who greatly admired Achilles, donned Achilles' armour and threw himself into the fight, killing many Trojans. When Hector, the strongest of the Trojan princes, saw Patroclus, he mistook him for Achilles. He burned for the glory of taking on Greece's mightiest warrior. Hector won the duel, slaying Patroclus. Only when he pulled off the dead man's helmet did he realise he had been mistaken – it was not Achilles. Still, he took the armour and wore it himself.

When Achilles heard that Patroclus was dead, his anger burned like fire in his veins. He forgot all about his argument with Menelaus and demanded that Hector meet him, man to man, in a duel to the death. Hector, ever the brave soldier, agreed, and the two men faced each other at the foot of the city walls. The fight was long and tough. Both men threw their spears and both met sword on sword. But Achilles had the Goddess Athena on his side, and with her gift

of strength, he plunged his spear through Hector's throat.

From the city walls, the Trojans begged for Hector's body to be returned, but Achilles' anger was still ablaze. He tied Hector to the back of his chariot and dragged him around the walls of Troy for all to see.

But even Achilles had a weakness. For when his mother Thetis had dipped him in the River Styx, there was only one place the water hadn't touched – where she held him: his heel. This would be his downfall. His killer, the cowardly Paris, was the most unlikely of Trojans to defeat him. He fired an arrow which the God Apollo guided into Achilles' heel. And so the man who thought he was invincible came to an untimely end.

The war continued to rage, with no sign of victory on either side. The Trojans could not drive the Greeks back to the sea, and the Greeks could not batter down the walls of Troy.

This problem was eventually solved by clever Odysseus. He was the King of Ithaca, and known for his cunning. Taking the Greek leaders aside, he whispered his plan.

The next morning, the Trojan look-out assumed his post on the walls, and was dumbstruck! Not only were the tents and the thousands of Greek soldiers gone, but there in their place was a bizarre spectacle: a horse, made out of wood and as tall as ten men.

Cautiously, a party of soldiers went out to inspect the strange object. Written on its side were the words:

A gift to the Gods from the Greeks,
in return for safe passage home.

The Trojans couldn't believe their luck. The Greeks had given up and gone home! Troy was saved! Whoops of delight spread through the city, and people made ready a feast of celebration. Everyone said they should open the city gates and pull the horse inside. It would stand next to their citadel as a symbol of victory. Only one voice spoke out against it – it was King Priam's daughter Cassandra. She had been given the gift of foresight by the Gods, but there was one problem. Though she could tell the future, no one believed her. She said the horse would be

the end of Troy, but her warning was ignored. They threw ropes around the horse's neck and dragged it inside the city. Night fell, and the people, drunk with wine and bloated with food, fell asleep.

No-one was awake to see a small hatch open in the bottom of the horse's stomach. Odysseus was first out of the hollow belly, then eleven others, all armed with swords. One man went to unbar the heavy gates. The Greeks hadn't really sailed away – they'd just retreated to a harbour hidden on an island called Tenedos.

Now the army was ready, waiting to flood into the city. The poor Trojans didn't stand a chance. The men were killed in their sleep and the women were taken prisoner. The Greeks burned mighty Troy to the ground.

The spell over Helen was lifted and she went home and lived a long and happy life with her husband Menelaus.

For Agamemnon, though, the ending wasn't so happy. While he had been away fighting, his wife Clytemnestra had taken a new husband, Aegisthus, with whom she plotted revenge for her daughter Iphigenia's

death. When Agamemnon's boat pulled into the harbour at Mycenae, Clytemnestra met him with open arms.

'Come, my husband,' she said. 'I have a hot bath ready for you in your palace.'

After ten years of fighting, nothing could have sounded better to the weary king. He slipped into the warm, soothing water. As soon as he lay down, a net fell from above, entangling his limbs. It was a trap!

'What's happening?' he cried out. 'Help me, my wife!'

Clytemnestra appeared at his side, but not to help. In her hand was Agamemnon's sword.

'This blade has tasted the flesh of many Trojans,' said his wife. 'Now it will taste yours.'

She stabbed Agamemnon over and over again, until the water of his bath was red with blood.

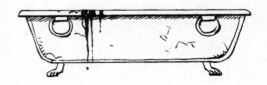

CHAPTER IX
THE VOYAGES OF ODYSSEUS

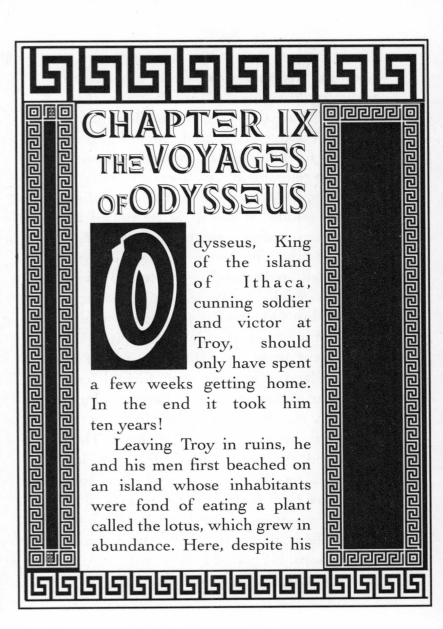

Odysseus, King of the island of Ithaca, cunning soldier and victor at Troy, should only have spent a few weeks getting home. In the end it took him ten years!

Leaving Troy in ruins, he and his men first beached on an island whose inhabitants were fond of eating a plant called the lotus, which grew in abundance. Here, despite his warnings, his men made the mistake of consuming the lotus plant. It made them forget their need to return to their native lands, and above all, it made them hungrier than ever for lotus leaves. Nothing mattered more than relaxing and eating the leaves.

Luckily, Odysseus hadn't been so foolish, so in the middle of the night he pulled his snoring men, one by one, back to the ships. He secured them to the rowing benches with rope, pulled anchor and began to sail away. Soon they awoke, desperate for the taste of the lotus, but Odysseus ignored their shouts and soon the island was far behind them.

The next night, the ship put ashore at another island. The men went to find food and shelter, and soon stumbled across a huge cave. They couldn't believe their luck. At the back of the cave was a flock of sheep. They slaughtered two and built a fire, gorging themselves on the roasted meat. It wasn't long before they realised their mistake. The ground began to shake, and suddenly a great shadow filled the mouth of the cave. It was a huge Cyclops. He glared at them with his one eye in the middle of his forehead.

'How dare you eat my sheep!' he bellowed. He stepped into the cave and pulled a huge boulder across the opening behind him. There was no way out.

Odysseus tried to explain that it had been a mistake.

'And who are you?' the Cyclops bellowed.

'I'm Nobody,' Odysseus replied.

The Cyclops, whose name was Polyphemus, and who was also a son of Poseidon, looked down and frowned. He picked up two of Odysseus' companions, one in each hand, and munched them down. After that, he lay on the cave floor, and fell asleep.

Odysseus and his men spent the night whispering to each other. They needed a plan of escape, otherwise they would all be gobbled up for breakfast. Odysseus could always be relied on to come up with a plan, and this time was no exception. They took one of the massive logs from Polyphemus' fire, and drove the burning end into the Cyclops' one eye as he slept. The giant howled in agony, and his shouts brought other Cyclopes to the mouth of his cave. But when they called to him in deep growls,

'Polyphemus, Polyphemus, what's wrong? Who's hurting you?'

'It's Nobody, Nobody's attacking me!' he replied. And so the Cyclopes, in confusion, marched back to their beds.

The next morning, Polyphemus was still recovering from his wound but threatened his problematic captives.

'Once I've let my sheep out to graze, I'll crunch through the bones of every single last one of you!'

Odysseus had to think fast. He told all his men to cling to the shaggy hair beneath the sheep's bellies. So, as Polyphemus rolled back the boulder and began to count out his flock, Odysseus and his band slipped out too and ran back to the shore. Only when they were safely back on their ships did Odysseus shout back insults to the blinded and fooled Cyclops. However, Odysseus would later pay for decieving the son of a God.

The ship was only a few days from Ithaca, when Odysseus and his men moored at Aeolia for the night. This land was ruled by a Aeolus, a man to whom the Gods had given control of the winds. In exchange for

Odysseus' wonderful stories about the Trojan War, Aeolus gave him a magical sack containing the winds that would help him get home quickly.

Odysseus used the winds sparingly, only opening the sack for a little while each time. But his men became jealous – they thought Odysseus was concealing some secret treasure in the sack. They were just a few hundred yards from the harbour at Ithaca, and Odysseus could see his wife Penelope and his ten-year-old son Telemachus waiting at the jetty. One of his men stole the sack and suddenly opened it. As he did so, all the winds escaped at once, causing a storm that blew the ships all the way back to Aeolia. This time Aeolus, angry at their stupidity, refused to help them.

Odysseus' companions rowed their ships between two headlands and anchored in a secluded bay, in the land of King Lamos. Odysseus himself, careful as always, moored up, and climbed the cliffs to look inland. Once ashore, his men met a young woman who claimed to be the King's daughter. She led them to her father's house, but it wasn't a

king who greeted them but two giants, a man and his wife. They were from a race called the Laestrygonians, a cannibal race. The giants grabbed and ate all of Odysseus' men who'd come ashore. Odysseus himself only just managed to get away with a small band of followers.

This small band landed at the island of the sorceress Circe. Lions and wolves roamed there, made tame under her powerful spells. She offered Odysseus' men food and wine and they feasted greedily. But one by one they felt their bodies changing. Circe had enchanted their banquet with magical herbs. Soon they were no longer men, but pigs! Odysseus was one of the few who didn't succumb. The God Hermes had warned him of Circe's power and he ate a special herb called Moly, which protected him from her devious plan.

However, Circe refused to change his companions back into humans unless he stayed with her for one full year. With a heavy heart, he agreed to the bargain, even though he was missing his wife terribly.

After the allotted months had passed, and before Odysseus set sail again, he descended into the Underworld to seek the advice of the soothsayer Tiresias. Since trying to warn Oedipus about his fate, Tiresias had died and could only be found in the Underworld.

Tiresias told Odysseus that when he came to the perilous straits between the Charybdis

whirlpool and the sea beast called Scylla, he should be prepared to lose six men to the monster's gaping mouths or to lose all to the whirlpool. Tiresias also advised him not to touch the cattle of the Sun-God Helios. While in the Underworld, Odysseus also spoke with the spirit of his dead comrade, the warrior Achilles, who died at Troy. Still angry at having died by the arrow of Paris, Achilles stalked the plains of the Underworld, scowling.

Setting sail once again, Odysseus heard, on the breeze, the most beautiful singing he had ever known. It sounded like a chorus of women. But he had been warned by Circe of these Sirens, harpies who lured men to their deaths on the rocks with their beautiful singing. To protect themselves, he ordered his men to fill their ears with beeswax and to tie him to the mast of his ship, so that he couldn't steer towards the enchanting sound. The Sirens, bent on success with their murderous scheme, sang louder and louder.

Odysseus thrashed against his chains, cursing his men to free him. Finally, they left the harpies far behind.

Next the ship came to Charybdis. The whirlpool was famous for sucking ships down whole and spitting out dead and drowned sailors. Odysseus knew from Tiresias that he would lose all his men if he steered too close, so he commanded them to take the dangerous route near to Scylla. As the prophet had fortold, the six-headed monster seized a man in each set of jaws. It was horrifying to behold.

The battered and distraught crew staggered ashore on the island of Thrinacia, where the cattle of the Sun-God Helios grazed by the shore. The crew, starving and desperate after their wearying journey, ignored Odysseus' orders and slaughtered some of Helios' cattle to roast over the fire. It was a mistake that Helios could not forgive. When the ship set out the next morning, Helios went to Zeus to tell him of the insult. Zeus readied one of his thunderbolts and hurled it at Odysseus' vessel, smashing it to pieces. All of the remaining crew drowned at sea.

All, that is, apart from Odysseus. Luckily he was washed up on an island that was

home to Calypso, a nymph who was one of the daughters of the Titan, Atlas. She fell in love with Odysseus and offered him immortality[1] if he stayed with her. For seven years he did so. He had no choice, for no ships or sailors came to Calypso's shores. Each night he longed to see his home at Ithaca, and his beloved wife. Even some of the Gods of Olympus felt sorry for him, and so they sent Hermes, their messenger, to speak with Calypso. With great sorrow, she agreed to let Odysseus go.

And so, Odysseus put out from Calypso's island on a small raft, only to be tossed around wildly by Poseidon's angry waves, and scorched by Helios' livid sun. When he eventually arrived back at the beaches of Ithaca, ten years had passed since the end of the Trojan war, and ten more since he had originally set out.

Meanwhile, all had not been well on Ithaca. Believing Odysseus to be lost at sea, suitors[2] had gathered at his palace, eager for his widow Penelope's hand. What they really wanted was the treasures and rich land that

1. *Everlasting life.*
2. *Men who all wish to marry a woman.*

came with her. When Odysseus returned to Ithaca, they were all living in his palace, eating the kitchens bare and drinking the cellars dry. Odysseus' young son Telemachus was no match for them. Penelope had managed to put all her suitors off thus far with a clever trick. She told them she was weaving a burial shroud for Odysseus' aged father, Laertes, and that she would marry one of them when it was finished. Each day she sat at her loom, but each night she secretly unstitched the garment. But the men's patience wore thin.

When Odysseus finally arrived at the palace, Goddess Athena disguised him as a beggar. At first, only his faithful old dog recognised him, but then his aged nurse, when washing his feet, realised his true identity. Finally he revealed his true self to both his wife and his son. Together they hatched a plan to see off the greedy suitors.

The next day, Penelope called them all together in the banqueting hall and set a challenge. She said that whoever could string[1] Odysseus' great bow, and fire an

---

1. *Attach the bowstring and tighten it.*

arrow through the loops of twelve axe handles, would be her husband. It was a difficult task requiring great strength and accuracy. One by one, the men tried and failed. Finally, a beggar stepped up, and performed the feat with ease. Then he whipped off his disguise and revealed that he was, in fact, Odysseus.

'You've pestered my wife, eaten all my food, and abused my kingdom,' he said. 'Now meet your end!' Odysseus and his son killed all of the suitors in a frenzy of anger. With that Odysseus' twenty-year quest came to a violent and vengeful end.

CHAPTER X
THE SONS WHO FLEW too HIGH

Phaeton and the Chariot of the Sun

Phaeton was out hunting rabbits with his friends on a hot afternoon. He pointed to the sky.

'There goes my father, the God Helios. His chariot draws the sun across the skies. Without him, we would forever be in darkness.'

Most of the time, Phaeton's friends just shook their heads and ignored him, but today, his best friend Timon decided he'd simply had enough.

'Will you stop talking nonsense, Phaeton,' he said.

No one had ever challenged Phaeton about his father before, and it angered him. He threw down his sling,[1] and launched himself at Timon.

'How dare you speak about my father like that!' he shouted.

Timon and Phaeton rolled about on the ground fighting, until their other friends stepped in to pull them apart. Both Timon and Phaeton were covered in scratches and their clothes were torn.

'You're mad!' said Timon. 'Your father is no more a God than mine is Zeus himself.'

When Phaeton arrived home that evening, his mother Clymene took one look at him and knew he'd been scrapping. As she set about mending his clothes, he told her what had happened.

'You silly boy!' she said.

1. *A weapon, often used in hunting, that consists of a small pouch in the middle of two lengths of cord. The hunter would place a pebble in the pouch, then swing the sling around his head to generate speed. Releasing one end of the cord caused the pebble to fly out.*

Phaeton sulked for a while. 'But is it true?' he asked. 'Or have you been lying to me all this time?'

Clymene told Phaeton that it was true, but that if he needed proof, he should go to his father directly. She told her son how to get to Helios' Golden Palace, and Phaeton set out to meet his father. He walked through the night and arrived at the palace a little before dawn. He was taken straight to Helios' throne room. Phaeton had to shield his eyes, because his father glittered like dazzling white flame.

'Greetings, my son!' bellowed Helios. 'How can I oblige you?'

'I need proof that you are really my father.'

'Well, that's easy. Ask for any one wish, and I will grant it for you. I give you my promise by the River Styx.'

Phaeton thought long and hard.

'I'd like to ride your chariot of the sun for a day,' he said. 'That will show Timon.'

Helios said it was far too dangerous, but Phaeton insisted, and a God's promise, by the River Styx, could not be broken.

It was almost time for the sun to rise, so Helios took his son to the stables where the horses were being yoked to the chariot. Phaeton gasped when he saw the powerful beasts, and the enormous sun glowing at the back of the chariot.

'You must be careful!' warned Helios, as he placed the reins in the boy's hands. 'The horses are wilful. You must hold tight and steer a middle way. Not too high or too low.' He begged his son to reconsider, but Phaeton was determined. As the stable doors opened, he waved goodbye to his father and cracked the reins. The horses bolted out.

At first it seemed easy. The horses churned the air with their hooves, pulling the chariot higher. Phaeton whooped with joy as the wind rushed through his hair. At midday they reached the highest point in the sky and it was time to steer back. Phaeton tugged on the reins, but nothing happened. He tried shouting to the horses: 'Stop!' But they continued to pull upwards. The clouds disappeared beneath them.

The Gods on Mount Olympus began to worry. They feared that if the chariot went

too high, they'd all be burnt to a crisp. As the temperature rose on Mount Olympus, and the Earth began to freeze, Zeus realised he had no choice. He hurled a thunderbolt at the out-of-control chariot, smashing the axle[1] to pieces. The horses broke free and the chariot plunged towards the Earth. As it shot over the land, it burned away trees, plants and rivers, leaving only sand and deserts.

Phaeton and the remains of the chariot plunged into a river. No God could save him, and he drowned. His mother and sisters recovered his body from the water, and mourned him. For many days Helios remained in his palace in sadness and the world waited in darkness, until one day Zeus persuaded him to take to the skies again.

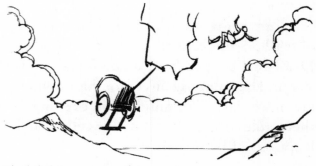

1. *The shaft that connects two wheels.*

Icarus and his Wings of Wax

After Theseus killed the Minotaur in its Labyrinth, King Minos blamed Daedalus, the craftsman who had built the Labyrinth, but who had also told Ariadne the secret of how to escape its maze-like corridors.

With his son Icarus, Daedalus was locked in a tower on the island of Crete. Their cell was hundreds of feet up, too far to jump. But Daedalus was a clever man, and formed an escape plan. Each day, he and his son would save a few crumbs from their supper to place on their window-sill. Birds would fly up, eager to eat the crumbs, but Icarus and his father would be waiting. They snatched the birds and killed them, plucking out their feathers.

After many months, they had a large pile of feathers under their blankets. But it wasn't Deadalus' plan to have a comfortable night's sleep. The cunning inventor had something far more daring in mind. One evening, after their guard had checked the cell, Daedalus leapt out of bed.

'Icarus, my son! Tonight is the night of our escape!' he said.

'But how?' asked Icarus. 'The door is locked. We can't go out of the window!'

'You're wrong,' said Daedalus. 'Light all our candles.'

Icarus did as his father asked, and watched as his father took two of the feathers. With a drop of melted wax, he stuck them together.

'We're going to make two pairs of wings,' he said, 'then fly away like birds.'

Icarus laughed.

'That will take forever!' he said.

'We'd better hurry up, then,' said his father. 'We only have tonight.'

And so, father and son sat on the cold floor as the moon rose across the sky. One by one, they joined the hundreds of feathers together. Just as the rosy dawn broke in the east, they finished. It would only be a short while until the guard appeared with their daily ration of bread.

'We have to hurry,' said Icarus' father, helping his son into his new wings. They felt light on his arm. 'Try them,' said Daedalus. Icarus flapped his arms and was surprised when his toes lifted off the ground.

'It works!' he gasped.

'Of course it does,' said Daedalus, strapping on his own wings. 'They don't call me the greatest craftsman in the world for nothing, do they? Time to go.'

Icarus was first to stand on the window ledge. It looked like a long way down. If this didn't work, he was sure to die.

'Just pay heed to one piece of advice,' said Daedalus. 'Don't fly too close to the sun. Stay near to the ground and you'll be fine.'

However, Icarus wasn't really listening. He was too excited. Taking a deep breath, he jumped away from the window. At first he plummeted with a yell, but then he lifted his arms a little. With a whoop of delight, he swooped into the sky, gliding on a current of air. He sooon found that he could flap his wax wings and climb higher. Behind him came his father.

'We're flying!' he shouted. 'I'm a bird!'

Together, father and son flew away from King Minos' prison tower.

But Icarus didn't listen carefully enough to his father's words. As the day wore on he climbed higher and higher in the sky, enjoying the sun's rays on his face after so long indoors. He thought he heard his father calling from far below, but when he looked down he saw only feathers fluttering beneath him. With horror, he realised that they were from his wings. He looked at them but the wings were already thin, where the wax had melted in the sunshine. He began to fall and he flapped harder, but to no avail. His wings were useless.

Daedalus tried to catch his stricken son, but he didn't make it in time. Icarus plunged into the sea and drowned.

CHAPTER XI
THE ANGER OF THE GODS

Prometheus

One of the Titans who escaped after the War with the Olympian Gods was a wily giant called Prometheus. He begged the King of the Gods not to send him with the others to Tartarus, and to let him live among men, and Zeus agreed. All he asked was for Prometheus to offer a sacrifice.

But Prometheus was devious. He laid out two offerings: the first was of the finest pieces of meat from an ox, wrapped inside the stinking lining from the ox's stomach; the second was the ox's bones coated in rich fat. Zeus, thinking the second was the better sacrifice, took that one. But as he crunched through the bones, he realised that he'd been tricked and decided to take his revenge. He didn't punish Prometheus directly. Instead, he took away the gift of fire from the mortals who lived on the earth, so they couldn't cook, or heat their homes.

'Why have you done this to us?' they asked the king of the Gods.

'Blame Prometheus!' Zeus replied. 'His insolence has led to this.'

So Prometheus was banished from society and wandered the earth with no friends. He grew to despair, and one day decided to take action. When night fell, he climbed Mount Olympus, and entered the sacred chamber where Zeus kept a fire burning. Prometheus took out a flaming ember, and carried it back down to the people of the earth.

When Zeus awoke the next morning, and saw mortals cooking their breakfast and

warming their hands by the fire, singing praises to Prometheus, he knew straight away who the culprit was.

He sought out Prometheus and inflicted on him the worst punishment he could imagine: he chained the Titan to a rock, and called down a vulture to gnaw out his liver. But that wasn't all. The Gods didn't give punishments that only lasted a day, a month, or even a lifetime. Because of their immortality, they preferred punishments that would last forever.

So each night, after the vulture had flown away, Zeus made Prometheus' liver grow back. Then, next day, the vulture would return to chomp away the new liver. Prometheus would have been there until the end of time, if a certain hero called Heracles hadn't saved him (see p. 88).

Sisyphus

Sisyphus was the Greek king who founded the city of Corinth. He was a clever and greedy man, piling up treasure in his counting house,[1] taxing his subjects heavily and stealing money from anyone in the land. His favourite trick was to invite guests to dinner at his banqueting hall, before poisoning them all so he could take their possessions. He would also hire bandits to attack travellers coming through his kingdom. He even used to steal from temples to the Gods.

But evil like this never escaped the attention of the Gods. One day Zeus' patience snapped and he decided he'd had enough. He asked his brother, Hades, to have Sisyphus imprisoned in the Underworld prison, Tartarus, and Hades agreed, only too happy to rid the world of such a monstrous man.

He handed Sisyphus, trembling with fear, over to the Spirit of Death, Thanatos.

---

1. *A building set aside for storing and counting wealth.*

Just as Thanatos was readying chains for Sisyphus, the king asked:

'Perhaps you should make sure the chains are tight enough by trying them on yourself.'

Thanatos locked himself in place, and showed Sisyphus that the chains were strong. Only when Sisyphus started laughing, and put the key to the chains in his pocket, did Thanatos realise he'd been tricked. The king of Corinth went to Hades and threatened him.

'Unless you release me from the Underworld, Thanatos will stay imprisoned.'

Hades didn't want to give in to this mortal, and refused. But with the Spirit of Death imprisoned, no other mortals on earth could die. It was an impossible situation. People got older and older, but never died.

There was one God for whom this just would not do: Ares – God of War. With Thanatos in chains, wars were pointless, as no-one on either side could die. So Ares himself came down to the Underworld and freed Thanatos, breaking the chains with his mighty strength. Now it was Hades' turn to

laugh. He took Sisyphus back to Tartarus himself, and set him a task: 'Roll this huge boulder up the hill. Once you manage to get it to the top, call me and on that day I'll release you back into the mortal world.'

Sisyphus strained against the rock for ten days and ten nights, and finally managed to push it up to the top. When he got there he was dripping in sweat and called for Hades. But as he did so, the boulder began to roll down the other side of the hill. By the time Hades arrived it was at the bottom again.

'Try again!' ordered the Lord of the Underworld.

After the second attempt the same thing occurred. Then again after the third. Sisyphus came to realise that he himself had been tricked. The task was impossible.

But he longed to be free to enjoy his great riches, so he never stopped trying!

Actaeon

Sometimes it isn't what you do that seals your fate – it can be what you see. The story of Actaeon is about being in the wrong place, at the wrong time.

Actaeon was a handsome young man in the prime of his life. He loved nothing more than to go hunting with his pack of hounds in the forests of Thebes.

One summer's day, armed with his spear and bow, he was in pursuit of a stag. The chase was long and hard, and in the end, he had to admit defeat. Nearby he could hear the rush of water, and parched with thirst, he followed the sound. Finally, parting some foliage, he peered into a grove. At first he saw a pool of water. But in the middle of it was a sight more beautiful than any he had ever seen. A naked woman was bathing in the cool waters, surrounded by nymphs. Actaeon could see that this was no ordinary woman, and could do nothing but stare in wonder. He should have turned around and left straight away, for the woman washing herself was Artemis, the Goddess of

Hunting. When she saw Actaeon, open-mouthed with wonder, she quickly covered herself up, and turned on him.

'How dare you, mortal man, gaze upon my beauty?'

Actaeon tried to make excuses, but the Goddess wasn't listening. She cast a spell on poor Actaeon.

'Just as you were the hunter, now you shall be the hunted!'

At first Actaeon didn't know what she meant, but then he felt a pain in his forehead. Reaching up, his fingers found a pair of antlers sprouting there.

'What's going...' he started to say, but then his tongue thickened in his mouth, and his lips had difficulty working properly.

His nose began to grow longer and his back legs buckled. He fell forward on his hands, but they weren't hands any more – they were hooves. Staring into the still surface of the pool, Actaeon saw not his own face, but the reflection of a stag.

He barely had time to register the change, when he heard the barking and yapping of his hunting dogs in the forest. The pack burst into the clearing and came straight for him. Actaeon tried to shout for them to stop but all that came from his mouth was the bellowing cry of a wild animal. With his dogs still running towards him, Actaeon turned and fled into the forest.

Fear drove him on as he charged through the undergrowth. He marvelled at his own speed and agility, but in time he began to tire. He could hear the gnashing of the hounds' teeth at his tail. Then he felt the teeth themselves. One of his most faithful dogs finished him with a fatal bite to the neck. This was a small mercy for poor Actaeon, the young man whose curious eyes innocently betrayed him.

CHAPTER XII
LOVE LOST AND FOUND

Orpheus and Eurydice

Orpheus was a lover of music, and a king in the land of Thrace. He fell in love with a maiden called Eurydice and asked her to marry him. All the kingdom rejoiced when she agreed. Preparations began for the wedding. Animals were killed for feasting, temples were garlanded with wreaths, and in the fields, Eurydice and her friends gathered flowers. But tragedy struck when a snake bit her foot. She screamed and fell into the meadow grass. As the poison seeped into her body, one of her friends went to fetch Orpheus. Alas, by the time he had arrived, she was already dead.

Orpheus wouldn't let himself admit that his beloved Eurydice was dead, even though everyone told him there was nothing he could do. Even as they buried her body, he still sang to her as though she was alive.

'You have to move on,' said his friends. 'Find another wife.'

But Orpheus had another idea. He descended into the Underworld, where dead souls roamed, and visited Hades and his wife Persephone. He begged the Lord of the Underworld to let him take Eurydice back to the world above, to give her a second chance of life.

'That's impossible,' said Hades. 'Death is final.'

Orpheus was not a hero in the traditional sense. He was useless with a sword and shield, and not at all brawny. He used a

different kind of weapon. Taking out his lyre, he plucked the strings and began to sing them a song.

The song he chose to sing told a story that was dear to Persephone's heart. For she didn't live permanently in the Underworld. She too had been collecting flowers one day, when Hades had caught sight of her and fallen instantly in love. He snatched her into his chariot and plunged back to his palace deep in the Underworld.

When Persephone's mother, Demeter, a Goddess of the Earth, had found her daughter missing, she had begged Hades to hand Persephone back. Hades felt pity for the grieving mother. He said that she could have her daughter for half of the year, and for the other half she would live with him in the Underworld. Demeter agreed. From that day on, Demeter lived in sadness when her daughter was with Hades, and rejoiced when she returned. That is why, Orpheus sang, for half the year the earth is dead and barren, and for the other half the flowers bloom and the trees swell with fruit.

His sad song brought tears even to Hades' old eyes, and he eventually gave in to Orpheus' wish.

'You can have your Eurydice back on one condition,' he said.

'Anything,' Orpheus replied.

'She will follow you as you ascend back to your world,' said Hades. 'But you must not look back. If you do so, you must understand that she will be lost to you forever.'

Orpheus agreed, and began to make the journey back towards the light, his heart

filled with joy. But gradually, doubts began to set in. 'Is my dear Eurydice really following?' he asked himself. 'Maybe I should check!'

He fought to keep his faith alive, but just as he was reaching the fields again, he couldn't help himself. He turned.

There was Eurydice, beautiful as the day he first met her. But as he looked, she began to be pulled backwards by invisible hands.

'What have you done?' she asked. 'Why did you look?' Her cries were swallowed by the blackness, and Orpheus never saw Eurydice again.

Narcissus and Echo

Zeus was famous not only for his thunderbolts, but also for the number of affairs he had with mortal women. Every time his wife Hera turned her back, you could guarantee that Zeus would be off somewhere else, wooing a different lady.

As time went on, Hera began to grow more and more suspicious, so Zeus had to find a way of distracting her. The answer he came up with was a beautiful nymph called Echo. When Zeus wanted to slip away, he would tell Echo to keep Hera busy, by repeating her last words back to her. Hera would say:

'Where has Zeus gone?'

And Echo replied:

'Has Zeus gone?'

Of course, this ruse could only work for so long, and when Hera found out, she was furious. She punished Echo by casting a spell on her. From then on, she could only repeat the words of others.

And so we come to the sad tale of Echo and Narcissus. Narcissus was known to be

the most handsome young man in the territory of Boeotia. Everywhere he went, the eyes of women followed.

But Narcissus was never interested in any of them, because he loved another too much: himself.

One day, while taking a stroll through the forest, he was spotted by Echo, who liked to spend time around the cool forest springs. But as soon as she saw Narcissus, love burned in her heart. She followed him, keeping at a distance, admiring his fine face and strong body. Hearing the crack of a branch behind him, he knew someone was following.

'Who's there?' he shouted. 'Come here!'

'Come here!' Echo couldn't help but reply.

'Show yourself!' ordered Narcissus.

'Show yourself!' said Echo.

When Echo finally worked up the courage to come out of the trees, Narcissus looked at her with scorn.

'How could I love you?' he asked.

Echo's tears welled in her eyes. 'I love you,' she cried.

But Narcissus was already gone. Hurt at such a cruel rejection, Echo prayed to the Gods: 'May he never find his love either, except in death.'

The Gods took pity on Echo and granted her wish. Shortly after, Narcissus came across a pool of still water and crouched beside it to drink. But then, in the water, he saw the most beautiful face he'd ever seen. Under the Gods' enchantment, he didn't realise it was his own reflection. As he spoke to the person beneath the water, saying 'I love you', he saw their lips move as well, saying the same thing back.

Finally, after many hours of looking into those deep blue eyes, he leant forward with a kiss. His heart beat faster as the water maiden leant up towards him. He reached out his arms to embrace, as did his new love. As he did so, Narcissus slipped into the water. Either he couldn't swim, or the Gods made the pool much deeper than he thought. In any case, Narcissus drowned in his own reflection, a fitting end for the man who loved himself so much.

And what of Echo? Well, for many years she roamed the rocky caves of Boeotia, avoiding people and crying her woes to the Gods. As time wore on, she didn't eat or drink, and slowly wasted away, until, one day, she wasn't there at all. She still lives now, but she can only be found in certain places. Go to a cave, or a rocky gorge. You won't be able to see Echo, but if you're lucky you will hear her voice. Just shout into the emptiness, and listen as she replies with your very own words.

FINDINGout MORE

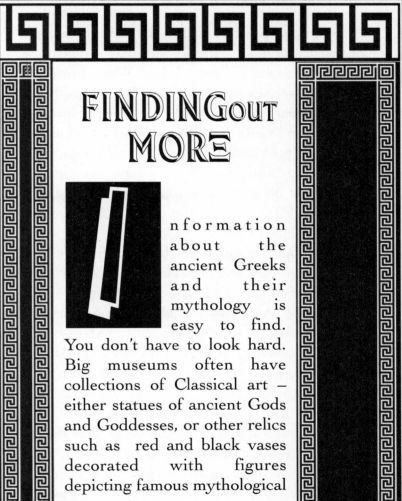

Information about the ancient Greeks and their mythology is easy to find. You don't have to look hard. Big museums often have collections of Classical art – either statues of ancient Gods and Goddesses, or other relics such as red and black vases decorated with figures depicting famous mythological scenes.

Also, many painters from the middle ages onward, such as Titian, Nicholas Poussin, Claude Lorrain and John Waterhouse, depicted scenes from ancient Greek myths, and several movies and TV programmes have been made which tell these timeless stories. Mythological themes are also popular in opera, and Greek dramas are still performed on stage today (though usually in translation!).

The physical remains of the ancient Greek civilisation can still be visited in parts of the world today. Temples, theatres and the remains of some other buildings have been preserved in Greece (especially the acropolis in Athens, where the architectural remains are extensive) and in Turkey, Syria and North Africa.

In any big library, you should be able to find stories in their original languages. Much of the work of the original Greek writers has been lost, but some has survived, and many of the stories are also told in Latin by later Roman writers. The Perseus

Digital Library (found at http://www.perseus.tufts.edu/hopper/) has hundreds of classical texts in the ancient languages or in translation. Homer, Hesiod, Plato, Apollonius, Plutarch, Ovid and Virgil are writers to look out for.

For a detailed introduction to ancient Greek myths in English, Robert Graves' *The Greek Myths*, first published in 1955, is very useful.

Modern authors have also been fascinated by the Greek myths. The writer Rick Riordan has written a set of children's novels that give ancient mythology a modern twist. His hero Percy Jackson (whose first name is a pun on 'Perseus') is a demi-god who undertakes adventures based on classical mythology. The series *Percy Jackson and the Olympians* includes five novels: *The Lightning Thief*; *The Sea of Monsters*; *The Titan's Curse*; *The Battle of the Labyrinth*; and *The Last Olympian*.

INDEX
OF PEOPLE + PLACES

A

Abderus (Ab-DARE-us) 84, 86

Achilles (a-KIL-eez) 126, 129, 130, 142

Acrisius (a-KRIS-ee-us) 103, 104, 112

Actaeon (ak-TIE-un) 167, 168, 169

Aeetes (ee-EE-teez) 52, 54, 56

Aegeus (ee-JEE-us) 62, 63, 66–69, 74

Aeolia (ee-OH-lee-uh) 138, 139

Aeson (EYE-son) 31, 32

Agamemnon (ag-a-MEM-non) 125–127, 129, 132, 133

Alcmene (alk-MEE-nee) 77

Althaea (al-THAY-uh) 117

Anchaeus (ank-AY-us) 118

Androgeus (an-DROJ-ee-us) 62

Andromeda (and-ROM-ee-da) 109, 110

Antigone (ant-IG-oh-nee) 98

Aphrodite (af-roh-DIE-tee) 23, 39, 52, 124

Apollo (a-POL-oh) 23, 46, 130, 185

Ares (AIR-eez) 23, 36, 54, 82, 86, 164

Ariadne (a-ree-AD-nee) 70, 72–75, 154

Aristophanes (a-ris-STOF-uh-neez) 17

Artemis (AR-tem-iss) 23, 81, 116, 121, 126, 127

Aspyrtus (asp-EAR-tus) 56
Athena (a-THEEN-a) 23, 38, 105, 106,
    124, 129, 146
Atlas (AT-lass) 28, 88, 89, 90, 144
Augeas (or-JEE-us) 82
Aulis (OW-lis) 125

B
Bistonian (bis-TOE-nee-uhn) 84
Boeotia (be-O-shuh) 178, 181
Briseis (bri-SAY-ees) 129

C
Calchas (KAL-kas) 126
Calydon (KAL-i-don) 115, 120
Calypso (ka-LIP-so) 114
Cerberus (SIR-ber-rus) 90, 91
Ceryneian (ke-ri-NAY-un) 81
Charybdis (ka-RIB-dis)
Chiron (KEE-ron) 33, 81
Circe (SIR-see) 141, 142
Clymene (klee-ME-nee) 150, 151
Clytemnestra (klee-tum-NES-truh) 132,
    133
Cronus (CROW-nuss)   26–28
Cyzicus (KYZ-ik-us) 41, 42

D

Daedalus (DED-uh-lus) 63, 64, 70,
  154–157
Danae (DAN-ay-ee) 103, 104, 111
Delphi (DEL-fee) 62, 78
Dictys (dik-TEE-is) 104
Diomedes (die-OH-me-deez) 84, 86
Dionysus (dee-on-EE-sus) 75
Doliones (dol-ee-OH-neez) 41, 42

E

Eros (EAR-os) 52
Erymanthos (eh-ru-MANTH-os) 81
Eteocles (et-EE-oh-cleez) 98
Euripides (you-RIP-i-deez) 17
Eurydice (yoo-RID-i-kee) 171, 172, 174,
  176
Eurystheus (ou-RIS-thyoos) 78, 79,
  81–84, 86-88, 90, 91
Eurytion (you-RIT-ee-un) 118

G

Gaia (GUY-a) 25, 27, 28
Geryon (GEH-ree-on) 87, 88

H

Hades (HAY-deez) 22, 28, 90, 163, 164,
     166, 172, 173
Helios (HEE-lee-os) 88, 142-144, 149,
     151–153
Hephaestus (hef-EYE-stus) 23, 83
Hera (HEAR-ah) 22, 32, 34, 37, 52, 44, 77,
     78, 83, 86–89, 123, 177
Heracles (HERR-uh-leez) 37, 39, 40, 43,
     44, 47, 77–79, 81–64, 86–91, 117, 162
Hermes (HER-meez) 23, 106, 141, 144
Hesperides (hes-PEH-rid-eez) 88
Hippodamia (hi-poh-DAM-ya) 105
Hippolyta (hi-POH-lee-ta) 86, 87
Hylas (HI-lass) 43, 44

I

Iolchus (YOL-kus) 31, 33, 34, 36–38, 57,
     58
Iphigenia (if-uh-gen-EE-uh) 127, 133
Ismene (is-MEE-nee) 98

J

Jason (JAY-son) 32–34, 36–38, 40–43, 46,
     48–52, 54–58, 67, 81
Jocasta (yo-KAS-ta) 93, 96, 98, 100

K
Kouretes (koo-REE-teez) 27

L
Laertes (lay-ER-teez) 116, 146
Laestrygonians (les-tri-GO-nee-uns) 140
Laius (LAY-us) 93, 96, 99

M
Medea (me-DEE-uh) 52, 54–56, 58, 59, 67, 68
Meleager (meh-lee-AY-guh) 117, 120, 121
Menelaus (meh-neh-LAY-us) 125, 128, 129
Mycenae (my-SEEN-eye) 125, 133
Mysia (my-SEE-uh) 43

N
Narcissus (nar-SIS-us) 177–179
Nemea (nem-EE-uh) 78

O
Odysseus (oh-DISS-yoos) 116, 130, 132, 136–144, 146, 147
Oedipus (EE-dip-us) 93-96, 98–100, 141
Oeneus (oh-NAY-us) 115–118, 121
Orpheus (ORF-ay-uss) 37, 50, 51, 171, 172, 174, 176
Orthrus (ORTH-rus) 87